THE ONE IN THE MANY: CHRISTIAN IDENTITY IN A MULTICULTURAL WORLD

EDITED BY
THOMAS R. THOMPSON

CALVIN CENTER SERIES
AND
UNIVERSITY PRESS OF AMERICA®

LANHAM • NEW YORK • OXFORD

Copyright © 1998
University Press of America,® Inc.
4720 Boston Way
Lanham, Maryland 20706

12 Hid's Copse Rd.
Cummor Hill, Oxford OX2 9JJ

All rights reserved
Printed in the United States of America
British Library Cataloging in Publication Information Available

Copublished by arrangement with the Calvin Center for Christian Scholarship

Library of Congress Cataloging-in-Publication Data

The one in the many : Christian identity in a multicultural world / edited by Thomas R. Thompson.
   p.   cm. —(Calvin Center series)
Proceedings of a faculty symposium on multiculturalism held at Calvin College, Apr. 25-26, 1997, at the conclusion of its multicultural year.
Includes bibliographical references.
1. Identification (Religion)—Congresses. 2. Multiculturalism—Religious aspects—Christianity—Congresses. I. Thompson, Thomas R. II. Series.
   BV4509.5.054   1998   261 —dc21   98-9626 CIP

ISBN 0-7618-1068-4 (cloth: alk. ppr.)
ISBN 0-7618-1069-2 (pbk: alk. ppr.)

⊗™ The paper used in this publication meets the minimum requirements of American National Standard for information Sciences—Permanence of Paper for Printed Library Materials, ANSI Z39.48—1984

Contents

Acknowledgments
    Thomas R. Thompson . . . v

Foreword
    Ronald A. Wells . . . vii

Introduction
    Thomas R. Thompson . . . ix

For the Healing of the Nations: The Book of Revelation and our Multicultural Calling
    Justo L. González . . . 1

Ungrasping Ourselves: A Kenotic Model of Multicultural Encounter
    Thomas R. Thompson . . . 9

Widening the Emptying: A Response to Thomas R. Thompson
    Leanne Van Dyk . . . 25

Racial Reconciliation in South Africa and the Theological Winds of Change That Inspired It
    Caesar Molebatsi . . . 29

Reformed Theology at Work: A Response to Caesar Molebatsi
    Glandion W. Carney . . . 41

Unity and Difference in Genesis 1
    Richard J. Plantinga . . . 45

Cultures and Communities of Higher Learning: Riding on the Bandwagon of Nonconformity
    David A. Hoekema . . . 51

Multicultural Openness and Victimization: A Response to David A. Hoekema
>   *Cornelius Plantinga Jr.*   63

The Comprehensive Plan: What Have We Accomplished?
>   *Steven R. Timmermans*   67

The Importance of Being Earnest: A Response to Steven R. Timmermans
>   *Michelle R. Loyd-Paige*   81

Pressing On: Some Concluding Remarks
>   *Joel A. Carpenter*   87

The Multicultural Year: A Retrospective
>   *Chris Stoffel Overvoorde*   93

Near Heroes: A Meditation for a Multicultural Year
>   *Thomas R. Thompson*   103

Appendix: Introductory Sections of Calvin College's Comprehensive Plan: (I) Summary; (II) Vision for the Future   109

About the Contributors   113

Acknowledgments

THIS BOOK IS largely a record of the proceedings of a faculty symposium on multiculturalism held at Calvin College, April 25-26, 1997, at the conclusion of its Multicultural Year. Beyond its many participants and support staff, that event owes much for its success to the vision, planning, and efforts of Steven Timmermans, Calvin's Dean for Instruction. It was also facilitated financially by a generous grant from the Jay and Betty Van Andel Foundation.

The record itself was made possible by the support of the Calvin Center for Christian Scholarship. We are grateful to the Governing Board for recognizing the importance of this project and for stretching its support beyond its normal mandate; to Ronald Wells, Director, for his wise oversight of this project; to Donna Romanowski, Staff Assistant, who lent much moral support throughout the editing process; and to Amy Bergsma and Kate Miller, Center Associates, who added their friendly faces and hard work to the mix and toil of preparing this manuscript for publication.

Finally, we are grateful to the broader College and Calvin community for a context that prizes pervasive Christian perspectives on life and that nourishes thoughtful Christian scholarship. We hope this book will aid our common quest to articulate and implement a biblical multiculturalism.

Thomas R. Thompson
On Behalf of the Multicultural Year Symposium Committee

Foreword

THIS BOOK IS a product of the Calvin Center for Christian Scholarship (CCCS), which was established at Calvin College in 1977. The purpose of the CCCS is to promote creative, articulate, and rigorous Christian scholarship that addresses important theoretical and practical issues.

The present volume is the result of the ideas and energy of the Multicultural Year Symposium Committee. The Symposium was the culmination of the yearlong celebration of—and thinking about—the meaning of cultural diversity at Calvin College. As anyone familiar with the work of committees will attest, it takes people with both ideas and staying power to make a committee's vision become a reality. Steven Timmermans was the motive force behind the Symposium Committee's mandate. Thomas R. Thompson was the person who made the Symposium a success, and who stayed with the project in the ensuing process of editing, for which he deserves much credit and thanks.

Calvin College is aware that Christian colleges have not been in the forefront of the discussion about the place of multiculturalism in the academy. We are further aware of the potential for politicization when cultural diversity is discussed. Nevertheless, Calvin College is proud of the energy, time, and money that went into the Multicultural Year in 1996-97. There were many insights gained that will change this college significantly. Some of those insights are distilled in this collection of essays and pieces that were presented on a weekend in April 1997. We are delighted to publish these proceedings in the hope that they will contribute a Christian voice to the ongoing dialogue about the meaning of cultural diversity.

Grand Rapids   Ronald A. Wells
December 1997   Director, CCCS

Introduction

THE QUESTION OF the One and the Many—of what unifies the diversity of the world and our experience in it, of what grounds and ensures identity in the seeming relentless flow of change—has long been a philosophical problem. And from the earliest stirrings of philosophy anything but a unity of answers has been given to this basic question. Parmenides, for example, opted for the One to the neglect of the Many, while Heraclitus declared that all was flux (Many) and void of any permanence (One). Socrates tried to establish universal definitions for society as a bulwark to the relativistic rhetoric and practice of the Sophists. His pupil, Plato, erected a lofty synthesis of these two, but tended to err on the side of unity and uniformity. Aristotle, on the other hand, made greater space for particularity. The problem of the One and the Many in its manifold forms has long preoccupied the human mind; it has remained the philosophical question par excellence.

It is still with us today. This question in its social form is even more acute given the breakdown of the modern world. The modern mind-set procured for Western civilization, for a time, a paradigm of universal truth, a metanarrative into which our individual stories could meaningfully fit—that is, as long as you belonged or attached yourself to the majority culture. So-called postmodernism has assaulted this modern ethos on all fronts, and in its social application has unleashed the phenomenon we call "multiculturalism." Multiculturalism most innocently is a celebration and respect of the diversity of peoples and cultures and cultural ways that inhabit our now-global society. As currently articulated and practiced in American society, however, multiculturalism appears a clear preference for the Many at the expense of the One, a preference often bolstered by many a sophisticated if not sophistical argument. What unifies this diversity of peoples and cultures and ways? Is there no One to which we can all appeal? Are we then reduced to standing around and bleating about our endless individual and group narratives to one another, stories that we are really telling past one another?

The relation of the One and the Many is also a theological question. And it is here that those who profess the Christian faith claim to have some additional resources to deal with this fundamental query. We acknowledge that the ultimate identity and context of human life is beyond the sheer ken of human reason (philosophy, strictly speaking), and that the knowledge of ourselves and of our world only truly comes to light in the knowledge of God.[1] Christian faith confesses its belief in the power and primacy of One and in the integrity of the Many: One God, our ground and goal of being, who is at the same time a rich diversity of Persons—Father, Son, and Spirit—the

---

[1] Cf. Calvin's comments at the beginning of his *Institutes* (1.1.1-2) that a knowledge of God is requisite to a knowledge of ourselves (cf. *gnothi seauton*) and of our place in the world—that is, human form and function.

Holy Trinity; one creation, a unified, yet gloriously diverse, space in which to live, indwelt by a Wisdom which prescribes healthy and uniform limits wherein humans can thrive in the responsible exercise of their freedom; one humanity, created in the very image of God, a unity of persons who come packaged in a diversity of gender, race, ethnicity, and culture (Acts 17:26); one renewed humanity, the Church, recreated in the image of Christ, professing one faith, one hope, one baptism (Eph. 4:4-5) as Christ's redemptive ambassadors on the earth through a variety of gifts, services, and workings (1 Cor. 12:4-6). It is the Christian story and its portrayal of the relationship(s) of the One and the Many that gives meaning and balance to our lives. Indeed, presupposing the light of Scripture, our problem is not so much that of the One *and* the Many, a theoretical quest, as it is in accounting for the One *in* the Many, a more practical quest.

The latter is certainly the case in respect to the social cast of this relationship. Christianity has not always fared well in representing this unity in diversity, in giving witness to true human identity (what Christian identity is supposedly about) amid its multifarious or multicultural forms of expression. It is an often-made remark that the most segregated moment—time and space—in American society is on Sunday mornings in our churches. It is to the overcoming of this lapse between theological theory and Christian practice that this volume is devoted.

More particularly, the majority of these essays and responses to them come out of a faculty symposium of the same title as this volume that was held at Calvin College, April 25 and 26, 1997, at the conclusion of Calvin's Multicultural Year, 1996-97. Calvin's designation of a Multicultural Year, a celebration of diversity highlighting for each of eight academic months a particular ethnic-cultural group and its heritage, was motivated most significantly by the desire to bring renewed attention and commitment to *The Comprehensive Plan for Integrating North American Ethnic Minority Persons and Their Interests into Every Facet of Calvin's Institutional Life.*[2] It is a plan that lays out both strategies and goals for making Calvin College a more diverse and multicultural educational environment than has been historically the case among its Dutch and Anglo constituency. This year-long focus on multiculturalism with a view to the Comprehensive Plan was all the more appropriate given that 1996 marked the ten-year anniversary of that plan's adoption and that Calvin was undergoing a considerable change of administration.[3]

---

[2] Authored by the Minority Concerns Task Force (Grand Rapids: Calvin College, 1985); hereafter, Comprehensive Plan. The introductory summary section of the Comprehensive Plan can be found in this volume's Appendix.

[3] Calvin College president, Gaylen J. Byker, was inaugurated the previous year (1995), while the Multicultural Year, 1996-97, was the inaugural year for Provost Joel A. Carpenter. For the former's vocal commitment to Calvin's multicultural goals, see his inaugural address, "The Embarrassment of Riches," in *Keeping Faith: Embracing the*

Introduction

The purpose of this concluding symposium was fourfold: (1) to celebrate the gains of the Multicultural Year—gains such as the increased awareness of and sensitivity to "the others" around us, the community contact made with various ethnic-cultural groups, and the sheer enrichment of learning about and enjoying the cultures and cultural arts that dot the landscape of God's world; (2) to wrestle with the heady issues of multiculturalism as they are being discussed and practiced in the broader society and as they apply to Calvin College; (3) to seriously assess where we were as a college in achieving a more diverse institutional life, especially vis-à-vis the Comprehensive Plan, which targets a variety of critical areas; and (4) to put Calvin College on record, especially its faculty (cf. faculty symposium), that we were committed or recommitted to the noble goals of the Comprehensive Plan to become a vital multicultural community and that we would continue to own the vision and spirit of the Multicultural Year, lest it become some rhetorical, romantic relic of the past.

The pieces of this volume will reflect this diversity of purpose. Most will have application to a wide audience on a variety of multicultural matters. Some of them will more narrowly reflect the struggle of one small Christian liberal-arts college with a homogeneous past to become a more ethnically and culturally diverse institution as it deems to befit life before the face of God. This latter is not a typical mien of Calvin College, whose publications have consistently been characterized by a panache of confident and rigorous Christian scholarship. We are not accustomed to such vulnerability, to airing or "publishing" our weaknesses. But our corporate life is also an open book, and here we readily admit our viator status, that is, we are still on our way. If other institutions can learn from our experience, then all the greater benefit to all. At the least, this volume puts us on record: Calvin College is committed to articulating and exemplifying a biblical multiculturalism.

The struggle admitted in these essays and responses echo Justo González's wise words to us in his address, "For the Healing of the Nations: The Book of Revelation and Our Multicultural Calling," delivered originally at our fall faculty conference at the beginning of the Multicultural Year. González takes his textual cue from Revelation 10:1-11, especially the image of John's eating of the scroll, a scroll that was sweet as honey in his mouth but bitter to his stomach (v. 11). The author warns us of the bittersweetness of

---

Tensions in Christian Higher Education, ed. Ronald A. Wells, (Grand Rapids: Eerdmans, 1996), esp. 18. For the latter's commitment to the goals of the Comprehensive Plan, see his contribution to this symposium's proceedings, "Pressing On: Some Concluding Remarks."

multiculturalism, how the ideal and rhetoric of it is sweet to the taste, but the actual working out and implementation of it is sometimes hard to stomach. We have placed his meditation at the beginning of this collection as a keynote.

My own essay, "Ungrasping Ourselves: A Kenotic Model of Multicultural Encounter," leads off the symposium proper. It is there that I initially provided greater context for the symposium in multiculturalism in general and the multicultural project at Calvin College, and so have introduced that theme sparingly here. My essay goes on to offer, on the basis of Philippians 2:5-11, a model of encountering the diverse other on the pattern of Christ's "self-emptying," or *kenosis* (v. 7a). This entails for us a self-emptying of those proud and boastful ways in which we attempt to justify ourselves, or securely grasp our identity, especially by way of confirming our lives with like-others at the denigrating and discriminatory expense of unlike-others. Leanne Van Dyk's response, "Widening the Emptying," provides a helpful broadening of this kenotic model to include those whose basic experience in life is not so much one of dominance and will-to-power, the sin of self-justifying pride, as it is one of passivity and powerlessness. Van Dyk suggests that for more marginalized persons—the socially disadvantaged, the poor, women, and racial and ethnic minorities—a kenosis or emptying of the sin of self-negation, not self-glorification, is the better prescription, which in turn provides us a more nuanced model of the imitation of Christ.

Caesar Molebatsi's essay tells a stirring tale of racial reconciliation. In "Racial Reconciliation in South Africa and the Theological Winds of Change that Inspired It," Molebatsi relates the checkered developments within the Christian church of his native South Africa that brought it to play a key role in postapartheid racial reconciliation. He also identifies the central theological themes and principles that emerged from intense church debate which inspire the present attitudes toward reconciliation in South Africa, making it a concrete and growing reality. The South African experience is not only widely instructive for us in the United States in our deliberations on and quest for racial harmony, but it has always been of special interest to Calvin College, an institution of Dutch Reformed ancestry. In "Reformed Theology at Work," Glandion Carney responds to Molebatsi, and reflects on some of these theological connections and points out that the Dutch Reformed Church of South Africa in its collusion with the apartheid government was in clear denial of its theological heritage. This is particularly important to emphasize since the power and social relevance of Reformed theology was a contributing inspiration to the very overthrow of that regime. Carney hopes that the latter legacy will be better remembered than the former.

In something of a theological interlude, Richard Plantinga's essay "Unity and Difference in Genesis 1," takes us right to the debut of the biblical narrative and to the theological resources implicit in the creation story for thinking about the One and the Many. There he sounds the themes of unity

Introduction

and diversity in God, creation, and humanity as theological terra firma for our approach to multicultural matters—themes that I have echoed in this introduction.

In his stimulating, "Cultures and Communities of Higher Learning: Riding on the Bandwagon of Nonconformity," David Hoekema poses, through a series of questions, the more general question of the extent to which multiculturalism in a Christian liberal-arts setting differs from that being peddled in the general marketplace of higher education. Warning against a trendy conformity to the latter, Hoekema offers insight and guidance into specific respects—such as concerning constituency, canon, and curriculum—in which these two agendas converge and diverge, yet argues for the uniqueness of the Christian multicultural agenda in the unique context of Calvin College. In his response, "Multicultural Openness and Victimization," Cornelius Plantinga Jr. garnishes Hoekema's position with his own insightful comments, a commentary that does not disappoint for lack of wit and winsomeness.

Steven Timmermans' essay, "The Comprehensive Plan: What Have We Accomplished?" launched the second day of the symposium, whose principal focus was the Comprehensive Plan. Timmermans reviews the four critical areas of this strategic plan—Faculty and Staff, Students, The Broader Christian Community, and Curriculum—assessing the degree of Calvin's accomplishments in achieving their specific goals. He offers an analysis of key issues that both foster and inhibit diversity in Calvin's institutional life, and concludes with his own recommendations on college policy and practice so as to facilitate the goals of the Comprehensive Plan. Michelle Loyd-Paige's response, "The Importance of Being Earnest," is a vibrant challenge to the Calvin community to be serious about its stated multicultural goals as she also reviews the critical areas of the Comprehensive Plan with some specific and pointed commentary.

Provost Joel Carpenter has the last word in "Pressing On." He highlights a number of contributions to these proceedings as particularly helpful and germane to the Calvin community. He also speaks *ex officio* for the College in ownership of the vision and goals of the Comprehensive Plan, but largely offers a word of encouragement to "press on" in pursuit of the multicultural community outlined by that plan which God desires for Calvin College.

We have also included in this volume Chris Stoffel Overvoorde's, "The Multicultural Year: A Retrospective," which approximates the report he submitted as the Director of the Multicultural Year, upon its conclusion, to the Multicultural Affairs Committee. This will give readers a brief record and flavoring of the various months and activities of this special year, as well as the observations, reflections, and recommendations of a long-term faculty advocate of diversity on Calvin's campus. The Multicultural Year was in some sense Overvoorde's swan song—his final creative work *at Calvin*— since this marked his last of thirty-one years as a professor in Calvin's art department. As a modest tribute to Chris' tenure of service and especially to his labors in orchestrating the Multicultural Year, we use the flower bouquet he designed as the visual symbol for the Multicultural Year as the cover image of this volume.[4]

Last, and certainly least, since we began with a meditation, we also conclude with one, a chapel meditation originally delivered during and for the Multicultural Year. In similar fashion it is our hope and prayer that all our thinking and doing, all our multicultural efforts would be enfolded by the inspiration and encouragement of God's Word. That Word frees us from our provincial selves and leads us into a province of people purchased by Christ from every tribe and language and people and nation (Rev. 5:9-10). May these essays contribute to that colorful goal.

Thomas R. Thompson

---

[4]During the Multicultural Year, the flower bouquet was accompanied by this inscription: "That They May Be One"/ 1996-97 Multicultural Year; along with this word of explanation:

> Diversity is nature's common language. From the songs of birds and the patterns of snowflakes, to the abundant variety in a bouquet of flowers, God reveals Himself by speaking through nature's rich diversity.
>
> Calvin College, on the tenth anniversary of the adoption of the Comprehensive Plan, has declared 1996-97 a Multicultural Year to celebrate the amazing variety of ways that we can express the unity to which Christ has called us. Each month a different ethnic group will guide us into new ways of praise for the gifts God has endowed each race, culture, tribe, and nation.

For the Healing of the Nations: The Book of Revelation and Our Multicultural Calling

Justo L. González

THE INVITATION TO speak at Calvin College's faculty conference came at a time when I was already overbooked and had firmly decided that I would accept no more speaking engagements. But this invitation came couched in terms that made it impossible to decline. For one thing, this is the opening of the first full academic year in which my friend, Dr. Joel Carpenter, will preside as provost of this school. It is difficult to say "no" to Joel's school, when in his previous position at the Pew Charitable Trusts he said "yes" to so many causes dear to my heart! But even more than that, I was told that this would be the opening event of what Calvin College has designated as its Multicultural Year. At a time when so many, even in some cases in the name of Christianity, are promoting cultural retrenchment and exclusiveness, Calvin's decision to celebrate diversity is particularly significant and worthy of any support I may be able to offer. Finally, the letter of invitation said that the purpose of this conference was "to begin the academic year in service to the Lord." Given these circumstances and guidelines, not only did I have to accept this kind invitation, but I also wanted to be sure that my reflections on multiculturalism had a sound biblical basis. A number of passages immediately crossed my mind.

An obvious text, and one on which I have worked quite often, is Acts 2, where Parthians, Medes, Elamites, and residents of Mesopotamia, Judea, Cappadocia, and so on, are all made to hear of the mighty deeds of God in their own tongues. While I shall not be dealing with that text, let it be said in passing: It is important to note that all these people were not given the power to understand the language of Peter and his companions. Rather, they were made to understand "in the native language of each" (v. 6).[1] At Pentecost, God confirms the translatability of the Gospel, which does not have to be heard in the language of the apostles to be authentic. I do not know if there was an "Aramaic-only" movement in the early church, but if there was, Pentecost is God's radical and final "no" to such a movement—and to every other similar movement, then and now.

Another text that is often cited in these discussions is 1 Corinthians 9, which contains Paul's radical claim to a freedom to become a slave of others: "For though I am free with respect to all, I have made myself a slave to all, so that I might win more of them. To the Jews I became as a Jew, in order to win Jews.... To those outside the law I became as one outside the law.... To the weak I became weak.... I have become all things to all people, that I might by all means save some" (vv. 19-22). This is a very significant and beautiful

---

[1] All Scripture quotations in this address are taken from the New Revised Standard Version.

passage about communication through solidarity, or perhaps about what missiologists call "accommodation." It is about the type of mission that will eventually bring about a multicultural church. But this passage is not expressly about a multicultural church, much less a multicultural society, so I pass this one up as well.

Of all the possible texts in the New Testament that deal with the issue at hand—the multicultural calling of the church in a multicultural society—there is none that is more explicit about the variety of peoples coming into the church, along with or including the specificity of their cultures, than in the book of Revelation. Indeed, seven times we find in this book, with slight variation, the theme of "every tribe and language and people and nation" (5:9, 7:9, 10:11, 11:9, 13:7, 14:6, 17:15). But we do not find that listing always in similar contexts—not even always in positive contexts.

There are in the Apocalypse some passages that are not very positive in their evaluation of the many tribes, nations, peoples, and languages. It is important to recall these, for otherwise we are in danger of romanticizing cultures and multiculturalism, and forgetting that they too have their demonic dimensions.

Take Revelation 11, for example, where John offers us the vision of the two witnesses. After these two witnesses have completed their testimony and are killed, John notes that "for three and a half days members of the peoples and tribes and languages and nations will gaze at their dead bodies and refuse to let them be placed in a tomb" (v. 9). In other words, while the glory of heaven is to be shared by a great multitude out of every tribe and language and people and nation, so also will the Lamb and his witnesses be opposed by others out of every nation and people and language and tribe. Multiculturalism may be an important trait in the very nature of the church, but it is also a characteristic form assumed by the powers of evil.

Revelation 13 makes that point even clearer. There John is speaking of the beast from the sea, and he says: "It was given authority over every tribe and people and language and nation, and all the inhabitants of the earth will worship it, everyone whose name has not been written from the foundation of the world in the book of life of the Lamb that was slaughtered" (vv. 7b-8). The glorious multitude dressed in white robes and singing hymns to the Lamb represents every tribe and people and language and nation. But so does the multitude that bows before the beast, adoring it.

Third, and finally, among these negative passages, is Revelation 17. This is the vision of the great harlot, wherein the angel explains to John that "the waters that you saw, where the whore is seated, are peoples and multitudes and nations and languages" (v. 15). If I had more opportunity, I would show that what this means is that the great harlot is rich, but she is rich because she sits on all these various nations and cultures exploiting them and having their wealth flow to her like many waters. Multiculturalism can also be a fancy name that cloaks old-fashioned exploitation.

What all of this indicates is that, even though there are great values in multiculturalism and in the affirmation of various cultures, we must not romanticize culture and multiculturalism, for they, too, are tainted by sin, and they, too, may be instruments of the beast and of the great harlot.

The increasingly multicultural society of the first century was not so different from the increasingly multicultural society in which we live. It too was a society in which people of different races and cultures met but where many resented multiculturalism, and even legislated against it. We are all aware of the tensions between Gentile and Jew in Palestine, and even between Judean and Galilean. In North Africa, in and around the city of Carthage, Roman mingled and clashed with Punic, and Punic with Numidian. In Egypt, similar conditions governed the relations among Romans, Greeks, Jews, and native Egyptians.

Keeping this in mind, let us look at Revelation 10:1-11:

> And I saw another mighty angel coming down from heaven, wrapped in a cloud, with a rainbow over his head; his face was like the sun, and his legs like pillars of fire. He held a little scroll open in his hand. Setting his right foot on the sea and his left foot on the land, he gave a great shout, like a lion roaring. And when he shouted, the seven thunders sounded. And when the seven thunders had sounded, I was about to write, but I heard a voice from heaven saying, "Seal up what the seven thunders have said, and do not write it down." Then the angel whom I saw standing on the sea and the land raised his right hand to heaven and swore by him who lives forever and ever, who created heaven and what is in it, the earth and what is in it, and the sea and what is in it: "There will be no more delay, but in the days when the seventh angel is to blow his trumpet, the mystery of God will be fulfilled, as he announced to his servants the prophets." Then the voice that I had heard from heaven spoke to me again, saying, "Go, take the scroll that is open in the hand of the angel who is standing on the sea and on the land." So I went to the angel and told him to give me the little scroll; and he said to me, "Take it, and eat; it will be bitter to your stomach, but sweet as honey in your mouth." So I took the little scroll from the hand of the angel and ate it; it was sweet as honey in my mouth, but when I had eaten it, my stomach was made bitter. Then they said to me, "You must prophesy again about many peoples and nations and languages and kings."

Clearly, this passage is patterned after Ezekiel, chapters 2 and 3, where the prophet is given a scroll to eat. If we compare this text with its literary background in Ezekiel, the parallelisms are obvious. There is no need to dwell on them here. What is more striking, however, is their difference regarding the eating of the scroll: while Ezekiel says: "I ate it, and in my mouth it was as sweet as honey" (Eze. 3:3b), John says: "it was sweet as honey in my mouth, but when I had eaten it, my stomach was made bitter" (Rev. 10:11).

Ezekiel speaks of a sweet word of God. For John, the word he is to proclaim is bittersweet. Why is that so?

If any writer of the New Testament was a Jew, steeped in Jewish culture and tradition, it was John of Patmos. It has been frequently pointed out that there is hardly a verse in his book that does not have some allusion to the Hebrew Scriptures. His Greek is full of Hebraisms, perhaps due in part to his greater familiarity with Hebrew and Aramaic, and perhaps as a result of his constant literary dependence on the Hebrew Bible. He quotes, not from the Septuagint version that all the other New Testament authors employed, but either from an unknown translation or from his own, which he prepares as he goes along.

John is well aware of the mission given to the prophet Ezekiel when the latter ate his scroll: Ezekiel was to speak only to the house of Israel, and they would not believe him. Now he, John, is not told *to whom* he is to speak, but *about whom*.[2] The difference between Ezekiel's vision and John's is not that Ezekiel is to go to Israel, to a people who understand his language, whereas John is to go throughout the world, to many peoples and nations and tribes and kings. The difference rather is that John is to go back to his audience, presumably the seven churches and other similar communities in Asia and speak to them *about* the many peoples and nations and languages and kings who are being added to God's people. And that is why the word of God, the little scroll that will be John's message, although sweet to the taste, is hard to stomach.

John the Jew; John who can quote the Hebrew Scriptures back and forth, apparently without even bothering to think about it, is given a message to proclaim to his congregations. His congregations are probably also mostly Jewish. Otherwise, they would hardly be able to understand this book he is writing to them, so full of allusions to the Hebrew Scriptures, and even to more recent Jewish traditions. And now he is told that he is to speak to these congregations, not just the word they expect—that those who are faithful until death will receive the crown of life (2:10), or that everyone who overcomes will receive some of the hidden manna and a white stone with a secret name (2:17)—but he is to speak to them about many peoples and nations and languages and kings. He is to speak to them, not only about how important it is that they be faithful in the impending tribulations and persecution, but also about "saints from every tribe and language and people and nation," those whom the Lamb has made to be a kingdom and priests serving God, who will also reign on earth (Rev. 5:9-10).

I submit to you that this is the most difficult aspect of becoming a multicultural church in a multicultural world. Bringing people in from other

---

[2]With the preposition *epi*, a genitive case would have meant that John was to prophesy *to* many peoples and nations and languages and kings. An accusative case would have meant that he was to prophesy *against* them. But the dative case, used here, means that he is to prophesy *about* them, as the NRSV correctly translates.

nations and tribes and peoples and languages is not difficult, as long as they are brought into the same church, dominated by the same nation or tribe or people or language. Throughout its history, whenever it has taken the Great Commission seriously, the church has been willing and even eager to prophesy to many nations, tribes, and peoples. It has also been willing to prophesy in many tongues and to that end missionaries have translated the Bible into thousands of languages and have even devised methods for reducing hundreds of languages to writing. We have certainly taken to heart the task of going throughout the world and preaching the Gospel to every creature. To that end many missionaries have devoted their entire lives, and even sacrificed them to death. For this task we continually collect offerings in our churches. And there are many in our congregations right now who complain that we are not doing enough of it and argue that we should try to recover our first love for missions.

Be that as it may, that is not what John is told to do in this passage. He is not told to go and speak to many peoples, nations, languages, and kings. He is told, rather, to speak to his congregations about many peoples, nations, languages, and kings, and he finds that bitter to his stomach. The communities to which he is writing are immigrant Jewish communities in Asia Minor, communities that have struggled mightily and for generations to keep their identity in the midst of a sea of paganism. And now he must speak to them, in the name of God, about the many nations and tribes and peoples and languages.

The difficult task we face as we seek to be faithful in today's world is not, as some might imagine, creating and sustaining ethnic minority churches. The difficult task is telling the congregations of the dominant culture about the many peoples and nations and languages that are also called to be part of the great multitude that worships the Lamb. This is especially difficult if those elements in the dominant community have not always felt dominant, if they themselves have long had to struggle against a sea of unbelief around them—a scenario not unfamiliar to the Calvin community. The difficulty lies in telling them in such a way that they realize that, no matter what they may have thought, their own people and tribe and nation and language is no more in God's plan than one of the many peoples and tribes and nations and languages whom God is calling to make, as Revelation would say, a kingdom of priests serving God (5:10).

It is easy to speak the word of a multicultural church in a multicultural society in such a way that it is sweet as honey in our mouth. And it should be. There is beauty and joy and fullness in many people's coming together out of every tribe and nation and people and language. But if we remain there, if somehow we avoid that part of the same word that is bitter to the stomach, we are not faithful to John's vision. The vision that John, the Jew, has is a vision of a Gentile church, a church where the Gentiles, the nations, *ta ethnē*, the *goyim*, would come and take their place right next to the tribes of Israel. All together would claim the ancient promise made to the people of Israel that they would be a kingdom of priests. That is a vision sweet as honey for it shows the fullness of the mercy of God, but it is also a vision bitter to the stomach because it shows that no people, no tribe, no language, no nation, can claim a place of particular honor in that fullness. And it is bittersweet because it involves radical change in the very congregations where John has served and that he loves.

And so it is with us today. The multicultural vision is sweet, but there is also a bitter side to it. There is the bitter side of having to declare that the vision of many peoples, many tribes, many nations, and many languages involves much more than bringing in a bit of color and folklore into our classrooms and our worship services: It also involves radical changes in the way we understand ourselves and in the way we conduct our business.

There is, however, another factor that must be pointed out. Although it is true that in a sense John's profound appreciation for his Jewish background may make it difficult for him to stomach the vision of many tribes, peoples, nations, and languages, it is also true, paradoxically enough, that he can be true to that vision only because he has that profound appreciation for his own culture. Similarly Paul is free to be a Jew to the Jews or as one outside the Law to those outside the Law because he can claim to be "circumcised on the eighth day, a member of the people of Israel, of the tribe of Benjamin, a Hebrew born of Hebrews . . ." (Phil. 3:5).

This is something I have come to understand as I have worked with people who are training to be missionaries among Spanish-speaking people. When I meet a candidate who appreciates her own language and culture, I know that she will be able to catch a glimpse of the beauty of my own language and culture. But when I meet a candidate who has not even taken the trouble to learn English properly, whose heart does not throb at the subtleties of Shakespeare or the cadences of Longfellow, I lose hope of ever being able to make him understand how I feel about my own language, about the rhythms that I heard in the cradle, or the sonnets that Lope de Vega addressed to the Crucified.

John of Patmos, who apparently cannot speak without quoting the ancient literature of his people, can understand both the joy and the pain of a vision where saints from every tribe and language and people and nation have been made a kingdom of priests serving God (Rev. 5:9-10). What we need today if we are to become a truly multicultural church is a working together or synergism of saints who own their respective traditions. We need a Jane Smith of Boston, who is deeply rooted in her Anglo culture and who shares and claims both the glories and the horrors, the bittersweetness of her tradition, to work with a Johnny Williams of Detroit, who shares and claims the glories and the horrors, the bittersweetness of his African American ancestry, alongside a Jan Vander-something-or-other, who shares and claims the bittersweetness of his Calvinist ancestry. We need these to work with Juana Pérez of Santa Fe, with John Silverfox of Tulsa, and with Jung Young

Kim of Los Angeles, all of whom share and claim the glories and the horrors, the bittersweetness of their respective traditions.

Together, and separately, we must each and all take the little scroll, that portion of God's message entrusted to us, and eat and digest it, and rejoice at the sweetness in our mouths, while we wonder at the bitterness in our stomachs; for we, like John, are called to go and prophesy again about many peoples and nations and languages and kings.

Ungrasping Ourselves: A Kenotic Model of Multicultural Encounter

Thomas R. Thompson

GIVEN THAT I am this symposium's lead-off batter, I will spend some initial time in providing some context for this event in multiculturalism in general and the multicultural project at Calvin College before I get to my paper proper, which is textually based on Philippians 2:5-11. The key notion for my essay is that of the *kenosis* of Christ, his "self-emptying" as recorded in Philippians. 2:7a. I will propose that this kenotic attitude of Christ is crucial for understanding not only personal encounter in general but multicultural encounter in particular. It is interesting that the word kenotic was misspelled in some of the advertising for this symposium as keynotic, as in keynote. While I do not presume to be giving such an address, I do think that the kenotic attitude of Christ upon his incarnation provides the keynote for his earthly ministry and for us in thinking about multicultural encounter. Hence the title: "Ungrasping Ourselves: A Kenotic Model of Multicultural Encounter."

Multiculturalism has become a pervasive and unavoidable topic of concern in society, the academy, and the church, particularly on the American scene. But what is it? As currently discussed, multiculturalism is not a discernible monolith submitting to easy or precise definition. It is, rather, a catch-all phrase for a kaleidoscope of themes, concerns, and practices, ranging from the highly theoretical, such as issues concerning epistemology and the sociology of knowledge, to the very practical, such as concerns over affirmative action, quotas, or canons of literature; from the philosophically sublime—what is the Self?—to what many consider the "practically ridiculous"—such as what is appropriate or "politically correct" to say in particular contexts.[1] One may think here of the sensitive language of "challenged," that overwrought word still somewhat in vogue, where, for example, it is not considerate to call people who are below average height "short." They are, rather, "vertically challenged." Those of us who have a harder time fitting into airline seats are "circumferentially challenged." White men, of course, are "saltatorially challenged"—that is, we can't jump. That students are "intellectually challenged" is no longer a compliment to the teacher. Now if all of this talk strikes you as petty and extreme, then you are quite possibly "multiculturally challenged." But then it is hard to tell whether that is something negative, to be criticized, or excusable.

---

[1] See, for example, the promiscuously inclusive range of "concerns and considerations, principles and practices, concepts and categories that now fall under the rubric of 'multiculturalism'" as delineated by editor David Theo Goldberg in his Introduction to *Multiculturalism: A Critical Reader* (Oxford, U.K. and Cambridge, Mass.: Basil Blackwell, 1994), 2.

A broad, good-face interpretation by its friends and advocates is that multiculturalism, quite simply, recognizes and celebrates difference. Multiculturalism prizes the particularity of diverse cultures and their distinctives in language, custom, and belief. Multiculturalism alerts us to the mélange of peoples and traditions that adorn our world and enjoins us to acknowledge the worth of the other as other. Diversity, equality, and inclusion are its watchwords.

Of course, in this sense, *multi*culturalism is a reaction to a "*mono*culturalism": that modern hegemony of the white European male. The claim here is that in this dominant *Western* culture, the voices, experiences, and perspectives of diverse other peoples, as tempered by their own historical, ethnic, and cultural matrices, have not been sufficiently acknowledged—a lack of recognition, it is observed, with sufficient testimony in the concrete social, political, and economic marginalization of minority peoples.

A broad, bad-face interpretation by critics of multiculturalism is that it celebrates diversity at the expense of any objectifiable unity or overarching truth. With the recognition of various cultures comes a tolerance of variables of belief, value, and truth—the axiological component of culture. Such epistemological and moral relativism has resulted in a societal identity crisis, a struggle to define those noble and enduring values that best structure healthy human community—a struggle captured, for instance, by James Davison Hunter's popular and conflictive title, *Culture Wars: The Struggle to Define America*.[2] Multiculturalism, according to its critics, entails a relativism that quickly degenerates into the balkanization of peoples and the politically correct clamorings of individual groups.

The association of multiculturalism with postmodernism has not escaped notice. Indeed, these two phenomena, both diffuse and difficult to define, nicely correlate, and together indicate a definite intellectual and cultural shift about us. Whereas modernity celebrated *uni*formity, a *single* universe of intellectual and cultural discourse, postmodernity, among other features, celebrates diversity, a *multi*verse of discourses, be it a polyphony of voices or a discordant Babel.

Within this social and ideological *wirrwarr* of multiculturalism, a jumble and muddle of issues and ideas, Calvin College is celebrating a multicultural year. What is "multiculturalism" within the Calvin context? Is this year-long event anything but chic or faddish? Is there perhaps a naiveté on Calvin's campus as to what multiculturalism may fully, philosophically entail, as some suspect?

Actually, multiculturalism should be given a more innocent reading at Calvin College, a reading quite understandable in light of its particular history. Given its roots in Dutch Calvinism, an ethnic homogeneity that served the college as a source of strength in many ways and for many years, Calvin has, self-admittedly, been slower at integrating other groups into its

---

[2]New York: Basic Books, 1991

Ungrasping Ourselves 11

institutional life—most particularly, racial minorities.[3] Acknowledging that the kingdom of God is better reflected by a community of diverse peoples (e.g., Rev. 5:9-10), Calvin adopted, in 1986, *The Comprehensive Plan for Integrating North American Ethnic Minority Persons and Their Interests into Every Facet of Calvin's Institutional Life.*[4] The Multicultural Affairs Committee (MAC) was thereby established "to function as the principal agent of the college in the development and maintenance of a genuinely multicultural educational community,"[5] a mandate considered critical to the mission of Calvin College, which reads in part:

> Moreover, the college strives for ethnic diversity, while also acknowledging its own ethnic roots. The goal of an ethnically diverse college community recognizes that the Christian community transcends cultural and geographical boundaries and [that] we live in a world community. Moreover, a multicultural community will assist in the educational goals of understanding different cultures and promoting understanding between people.[6]

From these statements of mission and purpose, it is clear that by the term multicultural the College has principally in mind the multiracial and multiethnic. It is a greater racial and ethnic diversity among the historically dominant Dutch ethnic majority, now perhaps better characterized as an Anglo majority, that is the principal goal of multiculturalism at Calvin College. The Multicultural Year that we are now celebrating is, on the occasion of the ten-year anniversary of the Comprehensive Plan and a new administration, an opportunity to both reconfirm our commitment to these noble multicultural goals and to assess our successes and shortcomings in achieving them.

Innocent though this may seem, suspicions still remain about the multicultural project at Calvin. Can one so facilely separate the multiracial and multiethnic from those larger multicultural issues that are belief- and value-laden and prone to relative interpretation?[7] Or does multiculturalism at

---

[3]For a good, brief history of Calvin College, see James D. Bratt and Ronald A. Wells, "Piety and Progress: A History of Calvin College," in *Keeping Faith: Embracing the Tensions in Christian Higher Education,* ed. Ronald Wells, (Grand Rapids: Eerdmans, 1996), 20-46. For the history of the Christian Reformed Church, the sponsoring denomination of Calvin College, see James D. Bratt, *Dutch Calvinism in Modern America: A History of a Conservative Subculture* (Grand Rapids: Eerdmans, 1984).
[4]Authored by the Minority Concerns Task Force (Grand Rapids: Calvin College, 1985); hereafter, Comprehensive Plan.
[5]*Expanded Handbook for Teaching Faculty* (Grand Rapids: Calvin College, 1992), Appendix BB, 259.
[6]Provost's Office, *An Expanded Statement of the Mission of Calvin College: Vision, Purpose, Commitment* (Grand Rapids: Calvin College, 1996), 35.
[7]Though the term multicultural tends to be a generic label at Calvin, quite synonymous with multiracial and multiethnic, one must actually reckon with these three (the racial,

Calvin College merely reduce to the proposition that people with different colored faces are to assimilate to a predominantly white, middle-class, "Christian" culture? Not only is there a suspicion by some (so-called insiders) that Calvin is naively playing with a value-laden pluralism which could, given time, erode its historic (even Christian) identity, there is just as strong a suspicion by others (so-called outsiders) that the dominant culture at Calvin— precisely because it appears to those within it so transparently "Christian"[8]— is too inflexible to embrace legitimate cultural variation in racial and ethnic minorities. As in society at large, multiculturalism at Calvin College poses its own questions of identity. Given these concerns, some broader discussion over this project is both timely and welcome. Hence this two-day faculty symposium, a fitting conclusion to Calvin's Multicultural Year, and intended as a way of celebrating its gains as well as articulating the challenges that lie ahead in bearing more concrete witness to Christian unity amid cultural diversity, particularly as it pertains to the Calvin community, and as mandated by the Comprehensive Plan. Perhaps we can also begin to address the concerns, even suspicions, over this project in respect to Calvin's historic and long-term identity.

Crises of identity are nothing new to Christianity, however. Indeed, the historic Christian Church has always faced an identity crisis as part and parcel of its missionary character. This crisis, more accurately, is twofold: It is a crisis of *Christian identity* due to the crisis of *being relevant* to the society or world in which the church lives and which is the object of its mission. On the one hand, to the degree that the Church attempts to become more involved in society and relevant to the problems and issues of the day, so as to contextualize and incarnate its ministry, the more it risks a crisis of its own identity. On the other hand, to the degree that the Church attempts to preserve and shore up its identity as Christian, the more it seems to risk relevance to the world. This "Identity-Involvement Dilemma," as Jürgen Moltmann labels it, is the necessary tension or dynamic of living out the Christian faith, of being *in* the world but not *of* it, of becoming *all things* to all men, without becoming *as* all men (1Cor. 9:22).[9]

The dangers are clear on both sides of this dilemma. The church or tradition whose predominant mode is that of conserving its identity loses touch with the world around it. It is prone to becoming an *ecclesia incurvata in se*, a church curved in on itself, an ecclesiastical ghetto, priding itself

---

ethnic, and cultural) as a spectrum of relations and determinations running from necessity to freedom, and which are capable of a complexity of combination in any one person. The point is, one cannot isolate the multiracial or the multiethnic from the multicultural proper, the latter of which is the most variable (free) locus of issues concerning meaning, value, and truth.

[8]Cf. Marshall McLuhan, who noted that environments are as imperceptible to us as water to a fish.

[9]See Moltmann's *The Crucified God,* trans. R. A. Wilson and John Bowden (New York: Harper & Row, 1974), 7-31, whose treatment informs my reflections here.

perhaps as the faithful remnant of a romantic past, the sole guardian of unchanging truth, accompanied quite possibly by those behaviors of the authoritarian personality. At the other end of the spectrum, the overly progressive church or tradition is prone to becoming an ecclesiastical Zelig (Woody Allen), accommodating itself in chameleonesque fashion to its changing Zeitgeist, baptizing any or all innovations in church belief and practice for the sake of relevance to the world. Both of these extremes declare their obsolescence as the *Christian* Church *in the world*, the principal redemptive agent of God's all-encompassing kingdom. And we can all think of varying examples and degrees of each.

For a tradition such as this one that prides itself on its ability to negotiate extremes (our "balanced approach" to all things) and that would want to compromise neither a strong Christian and Reformed identity nor an active engagement with contemporary culture, the challenge at hand is to articulate that identity in a world that is becoming more consciously multicultural, which is to say, to hone that identity in a multicultural way—affirming our oneness of *theological identity*, not above, around, or under but *in* the many.

Let me therefore underscore three reasons why the Christian Church and Calvin College must take multiculturalism seriously. First, allied with postmodernism, multiculturalism presents some serious intellectual and social challenges to Christianity. For any Christian tradition that claims to be culture engaging with a view to being culture transforming, we must engage this phenomenon, which is here to stay. Second, the fact that the world has become a global village entails that we must have the necessary intercultural skills to be able to deal gracefully and respectfully with various and sundry peoples. This is especially the case for our own society, given the "browning of America," where, by the most reserved demographic estimates, Anglos will be a bare majority by the year 2050.[10] Third, and most importantly, Christianity, to the extent it wants to live by the dictates of Scripture, has its own version and vision of multiculturalism that not only needs to be articulated, but implemented—that is, *lived out*. This as a preemptive praxis, or model for the world of how the Many can indeed be One, a healthy whole—a unity in diversity that according to Jesus' high priestly prayer in John 17 is the very condition of the efficacy of the church's mission (John 17:20-23).

This last point I am going to assume. The theological resources for a Christian multiculturalism are not lacking. That Scripture gives us a multicultural vision throughout is undeniable: The kingdom of God encompasses a rich diversity of peoples from every nation, tribe, and language—one people in a manyness of culture. One could refer here to the biblical survey of this multicultural vision by a synodical study committee of

---

[10] The 1990 census indicated: 76% Anglo; 12% black; 9% Latino; 3% Asian. Estimates for 2050: 52% Anglo; 16% black; 22% Latino; 10% Asian. From "The Numbers Game," *Time* special issue, *The New Face of America*, Fall 1993, 14-15.

the Christian Reformed Church, the sponsoring denomination of Calvin College, available in the pamphlet "God's Diverse and Unified Family."[11] Even now the Church universal is de facto multicultural, at least on a model of institutional pluralism. Does not this simple fact itself entail a mandate for multicultural encounter? So why are we, the Christian Church, still very much cloistered in our diversity? Why are we so fledgling, awkward, and ungraceful at multicultural encounter? Why so reluctant to cross the picket lines of race, ethnicity, or culture? And here I have begun my paper proper.[12]

Our problem, it seems, is not so much one of theory, or theology—indeed, we all theoretically embrace biblical multiculturalism and relish the rhetoric of diversity; our problem is, rather, one of practice: We seem, more than not, stuck in our rhetoric. So what might motivate us to a more multicultural practice and inclusion? To what could we appeal as an evocative motivator of multicultural encounter?

Permit me to invoke a venerable theological tradition and devotional practice, the imitation of Christ or *imitatio Christi*, as a serious goad to this goal. I would like to root the art of so-called multicultural encounter in the very life of Christ, and in this way make it a *discipline* of Christian spirituality, an imperative of basic Christian *discipleship*. WWJD—"What Would Jesus Do?"— is a recent and popular manifestation of this approach by way of the imitation of Christ. But even when commercialized in the selling of wrist bands, it is a principle of Christian practice against which it is hard to argue.

It would not take but a cursory review of Jesus' life to see that his ministry is peppered with multicultural encounter, and therefore wholly consonant with the grand vision of Scripture. The promised one, whose own genealogy includes ethnic diversity (Matt. 1:5), and whose birth is hailed by the wise Magi of other nations (Matt. 2:1-12), lived a life of servanthood in solidarity with the various outcast and marginalized, including, in the provincial Jewish society of his time, the ethnically diverse. Though he claimed to have come "unto his own," Jesus also ministers to many "others": to the Roman centurion (Matt. 8:5-13), the Canaanite woman (Matt. 15:21-28), the Samaritan woman (John 4:1-26; cf. 4:39-42), the Greeks (apparently,

---

[11] Grand Rapids: Christian Reformed Church in North America, 1996.

[12] That the universal church is de facto multicultural might suggest to some that it is already integrated, on the model of institutional pluralism. Can one, after all, expect every local church or denomination to be fully integrated in the same speckled ratios (all black, Hispanic or Korean churches, for example, reflecting a similar integrated constituency)? Certainly not—that would entail the homogenization of cultures and thus the defeat of created diversity. But even institutional pluralism ought to entail the working together of racially, ethnically, and culturally diverse churches, which requires a willingness and practice of multicultural encounter. Calvin College, an institution of higher learning, with a mission of serving all peoples, has rightly opted for a more local model of integration than to remain content to simply serve and reflect the majority culture.

John 12:20-22). He "talks and walks" an ethic of love that transcends cultural barriers. The parable of the Good Samaritan, for pointed example, prescribes the love of one's ethnically hated neighbor, like the Samaritans (Luke 10:25-37), an association and advocacy for which Jesus is derided. He himself is called a Samaritan and demon possessed in the same breath, parallel terms of denigration (John 8:48; see also Luke 9:51-56; 17:11-17). But like the book of Jonah (cf. Matt. 12:40-41), Jesus holds up other nations and peoples as righteous foils to his Jewish contemporaries (Matt. 11:20-21; 12:40-42). Jesus can do this, since he claims that upon his return he will judge all peoples (Matt. 25:31-46); and it is in this light that he commissions his followers to make disciples of all nations (Matt. 28:16-20).

Rather than elaborate and dwell on this clear pattern of multicultural encounter in the historic ministry of Jesus,[13] I would like to take a slightly different tack, and root the imitative impulse toward multicultural encounter in the very act of our Lord's incarnation as delineated in Philippians 2:6-11 and surrounding context. This passage, rich and sublime, most likely an early Christian hymn or *Carmen Christi*, describes the way of the preexistent Son of God into the world as a *kenosis* (v. 7a), a self-emptying, an act and attitude of self-denial and humility that, in turn, provides the keynote of Jesus' earthly ministry. It is this *kenosis*, this self-emptying, this kenotic attitude of Christ to enter into the life of "the Other" that undergirds Paul's appeal (or paraenesis) to the Philippians for Christian unity—his imperative that they live together in harmony and one accord. I would like to briefly explicate this passage in its immediate context (1:27-2:5) as an evocative model for multicultural encounter, a kenotic model of multicultural encounter, which when we read between its terse lines, biblically and theologically, may very well give us insight into what hinders our grace and facility in this area.

We must first note that the Philippian church itself suffers discord, disunity (Phil. 2:2-4; 4:2). In the epistle, this appears more a function of rivaling ideologies to Paul's gospel and instruction than anything else. Such division may also be fueled by ethnic tensions, however, since Philippi was a mix, at the least, of native Thracians, Roman colonists, and Jews, the latter of which, there is good evidence, were the brunt of anti-Semitic attitudes (cf. Acts 16:20-21), and whose presence in the Philippian church may be largely responsible for its experience of hostility and persecution (1:28-30).[14]

In the midst of these dangers of division from within and persecution from without, Paul exhorts the Philippians to be steadfast and courageous by standing "firm in *one spirit*, contending as *one person* (literally, "one soul") for the faith of the gospel" (1:27). He continues that appeal in chapter 2, encouraging those who, understatedly, have *any* union with Christ, even the

---

[13] I take these encounters recorded in Scripture as *representative* of Jesus' ministry and not historically exhaustive.

[14] See Ralph P. Martin, *Philippians*, The New Century Bible Commentary (Grand Rapids: Eerdmans, 1976), 2-7.

slightest bit, to be "*like-minded*, having the *same love*, being *one in spirit* (literally, "one in soul") and purpose"(2:2).[15] How are they to implement such unity? Humility is the key, since it is the antidote to self-centeredness, the chief obstacle to unity. "Do nothing out of selfish ambition or vain conceit," says Paul, "but in humility consider others better than yourselves" (2:3), which, he goes on to clarify, means looking not only to one's own interests but also to the interests of others (2:4). And for this selfless and humble habit of mind, Paul appeals to the very example of Christ: "Your attitude should be the same as that of Christ Jesus" (2:5). It is an attitude the apostle then illustrates by quoting, with slight amendment, a hymn of early Christian worship, a Christological ode that praises the church's Lord by recalling his way of humiliation and exaltation, that one

> [6]Who, being in very nature God,
> did not consider equality with God
> something to be grasped,
> [7]but made himself nothing,
> taking the very nature of a servant,
> being made in human likeness.
> [8]And being found in appearance as a man,
> he humbled himself
> and became obedient to death—
> even death on a cross!
> [9]Therefore God exalted him to the highest place
> and gave him the name that is above every name,
> [10]that at the name of Jesus every knee should bow,
> in heaven and on earth and under the earth,
> [11]and every tongue confess that Jesus Christ is Lord,
> to the glory of God the Father.[16]

While this passage is familiar enough to most of us, it is also regarded as one of the most difficult pericopes in the New Testament to exegete.[17] This is

---

[15]All Scripture quotations are taken from the New International Version. Emphases are mine.

[16]It is generally held that v. 8d, "even death on a cross," is Paul's own addition to this hymn.

[17]States Ralph P. Martin, renowned watcher and expositor of this passage: "There are certain passages of Scripture which both provoke and baffle study. Philippians ii. 5-11 is one such section, as all who have tried their hand at its interpretation know full well." Further, states Martin: "If A. B. Bruce in 1876 could write of the diversity of opinion [on this text] as 'enough to fill the student with despair, and to afflict him with intellectual paralysis,' that sombre appraisal of the situation is even more confirmed in 1967"—the original copyright date of Martin's significant study, *Carmen Christi: Philippians 2:5-11 in Recent Interpretation and in the Setting of Early Christian*

especially the case for verses 6 and 7, which will preoccupy our attention, and for which purposes I would like to give this working translation:

> 6a Who being in the form of God,
> b did not consider equality with God
>   something to be grasped (*harpagmon*),
> 7a but he emptied (*ekenosen*) himself,
> b taking the very nature of a servant,
> c being made in human likeness.

My contention is that if we do our homework well, fleshing out these verses biblically, we will uncover not only a Christological model of personal encounter in general, but also, by reading more theologically between their lines, a model of multicultural encounter by application, one whose *leitmotif* is that of *kenosis*—"self emptying"—hence a kenotic model of multicultural encounter.[18] This model, moreover, I will contend, goes to the very heart of the church's identity-involvement dilemma.

The passage begins (6a) from the point of view of the preexistent Son "in the form of God" (*en morphē theou*), that is, his equality with God the Father (cf. NIV: "in very nature God"), since the hymn as a whole traces the drama of the way of Christ (*Weglied*) in his descent, humiliation, and exaltation.[19] We are then immediately confronted with this enigmatic assertion: Though being equal to God, Christ "did not consider equality with God something to be grasped" (6b); instead, "he emptied himself, taking the very nature of a servant" (7a & b). What would it mean for someone who is already equal to God to grasp (*harpagmos*) after equality with God? How are we to understand such an assertion and imagery?

Worship, rev. ed. (Grand Rapids: Eerdmans, 1983), vii, 20. Martin himself, for a number of reasons, disputes the so-called ethical interpretation of Phil. 2:5-11 and doubts that this passage enjoins an imitation of Christ as is clearly conveyed by the NIV translation of verse 5 (see xii-xix, 68-74, 84-88). For him the heart of this text is "Christ's present lordship set under the cross" (xvii). But this seems to me to embrace a false dichotomy. Even if the center of gravity of this text is the historical-redemptive lordship of Christ who triumphs through the cross, this does not preclude an imitation of his way of triumph—namely, through self-sacrifice (kenosis), and Martin seems to admit as much on occasion (e.g., xvi). The theme of imitation is even more evident if there is a distinct Adam motif in this text, which I will argue below that there is.

[18] This is, therefore, an exegetical *and* theological analysis of this passage. While the exegetical treatment can only be selective, and will be lightly documented in footnotes, the broader theological analysis will find more play and emphasis in application to the multicultural topic at hand.

[19] I agree with that wide range of commentators, including Martin, who see in *en morphē theou* a clear affirmation of Christ's personal preexistence. See Martin, *Carmen Christi*, 99-133, esp. 119.

Let me cut to the quick of my interpretive angle. I am in agreement with those commentators who contend that the language and imagery of the Philippians hymn, especially the difficult verses of 6 and 7, cannot be fully appreciated, or correctly interpreted for that matter, apart from seeing in them a conscious play on the Adam motif.[20] Paul, we know from other passages (Rom. 5:12-21; 1Cor. 15:20-22; 45-50), contrasts Adam, as the first man, with Christ, as the second man or the last man. These two personalities face off as the great representatives of two epochs or ages: The first Adam brought death through disobedience, the second Adam life through obedience (see Rom. 5:18-19). This same contrast makes terrific sense of the difficult exegetical waters of the Philippians hymn. Compare, for instance, the following chart:

Adam	Christ
Made in the divine image thought it a prize to be grasped at to be as God; and aspired to a reputation	Being the image of God thought it not a prize to be grasped at to be as God; and made himself of no reputation
and spurned being God's servant seeking to be in the likeness of God; and being found in fashion as a man (of dust, now doomed), he exalted himself, and became disobedient unto death. He was condemned and disgraced.	and took upon Him the form of a servant and was made in the likeness of men; and being found in fashion as a man (Rom. viii. 3), He humbled Himself, and became obedient unto death. God highly exalted Him and gave Him the name and rank of Lord.[21]

Adam, after all, was also "in the *form* of God" (6a') by virtue of possessing the *glory* of being created in God's *image*, form (*morphē*), image (*eikon*), and glory (*doxa*) being semantic equivalents in Pauline usage and conceptuality.[22] But though in the form or glorious image of God, Adam, for one reason or another, grasped (*harpagmos*) above himself and his

---

[20]See Martin, *Carmen Christi*, xx, 125, 130, 158-59, 161-64, 210, 293. Oscar Cullmann, Martin notes, "puts it categorically: 'Except for this background of the Pauline teaching of the two Adams' this verse (ii. 6) 'is scarcely intelligible'" (162).
[21]Taken from Martin, *Carmen Christi*, 163-64.
[22]See Herman Ridderbos, *Paul: An Outline of His Theology*, trans. John Richard De Witt (Grand Rapids: Eerdmans, 1975), 73-74; and Martin, *Carmen Christi*, 102-120.

creaturehood at equality with God (6b'), as prompted by the Tempter's enticing words: "you will be like God" (Gen. 3:5). In the attempt to make himself something (7a')—indeed, God (7c')—he rejected his servant role (7b'); though he found himself in fashion as a man of dust (8a'), he exalted himself (8b'), and became disobedient unto death (8c'). Adam was condemned and disgraced (9-11').

Christ, on the other hand, though being *the* image of God, possessing eternal glory with God the Father (6a),[23] did not consider his equality with God something to be grasped (*harpagmos*) in the sense of "jealously guarded" or "hoarded for its own sake" (*res rapta*) (6b).[24] He was willing to empty himself of his glory and status and prerogatives (7a)[25] and to take on the very nature of a servant (7b) by being made in human likeness (7c). This kenotic movement continues in his earthly ministry of servanthood (8a) as he humbles himself (8b) and becomes obedient to death (8c), only thereby to be exalted as Lord and given the repute and name above all names (9-11).

In this way Christ "recapitulates" Adam's vocation as the image of God, to borrow a term and favorite theme of Irenaeus (*recapitulatio*). That is, he "sums up" Adam's task, "going over the same ground" as Adam, but with the opposite outcome. Christ retraces Adam's life—his experiences, choices, temptations—and overcomes and reverses that way of disobedience, defeat, and death by virtue of his obedient life—a rich, rich vein for our meditation.[26]

Given this first Adam-second Adam interpretive framework, I would like to read a little more theologically between the lines of verses 6 and 7, so as to develop a kenotic model of multicultural encounter.

What is our (Adamic) grasping after God to which the example of Christ provides the antidote? What is our fundamental and perennial sin? Well the question of original sin is a large one, and its efficient cause must certainly remain a mystery—a mystery of human freedom—for to explain it is to exculpate ourselves before God. But given its fact, and the temptation that

---

[23] Cf. Heb. 1:3: "The Son is the radiance of God's glory and the exact representation of his being."

[24] States Martin: "The term *harpagmos* poses one of the most thorny questions in the whole field of New Testament exegesis," *Carmen Christi*, 134. Given the supposition of Christ's preexistence and of the equivalence of "form of God" and "equality with God" in verse 6, I opt for the *res rapta* sense of this term: Christ's equality with God was something that he already possessed, but he chose not to grasp it (*harpagmos*) or "jealously guard" it in lieu of the Incarnation and its hard way of service.

[25] This passage has given rise to "kenotic Christologies" that flourished especially in the nineteenth century and that held that Christ's kenosis involved the self-emptying or self-limitation of divine powers and attributes. Given the purpose of this paper, I need not broach the kenosis question in respect to those metaphysical dimensions.

[26] To my knowledge, however, Irenaeus does not make use of Philippians 2:5-11 in his elaboration of *recapitulatio*, though his pervasive treatment of this seminal Pauline framework can only serve to reinforce its presence in the Philippians hymn.

provoked it, we may note a few things about the basic character of primal human sin.

Reinhold Niebuhr, in his classic *The Nature and Destiny of Man*, offers us some pertinent reflections here.[27] Standing at the juncture—indeed, paradox—of nature and spirit, finiteness and freedom, the basic human condition is one of anxiety.[28] Anxiety, or insecurity, is not sin itself but is the "precondition of sin"[29] and a "source of temptation" when this condition is "falsely interpreted"[30]—that is, when basic human security is sought outside of dependence upon the Creator, which is an act and attitude of unbelief.[31] States Niebuhr: "Man is insecure and involved in natural contingency; he seeks to overcome his insecurity by a will-to-power which overreaches the limits of human creatureliness."[32] Accordingly, "His sin and fall consists in his effort to transcend his proper state and to become like God."[33]

To become like God, *sicut deus*, is to transgress our limit, to declare our independence, to become our own creators in rebellion of our creatureliness, and to live out of our own resources and selves. That is the knowledge of good and evil, notes Dietrich Bonhoeffer.[34] To know good and evil is to become like God (Gen. 3:22)—a self-determining creator and judge of our own life, acting out of our own potentiality and power, becoming our own standard and reference of right and wrong, good and bad. Though already created in the image and likeness of God, we have grasped at yet another likeness to God and divinized ourselves; we have become gods against God.

A shorthand way of talking about this original sin of self-deification, it seems to me, is self-justification, to which a principal teaching of the Reformation provides an appropriate antidote. In rejecting God, human insecurity seeks its own security and resting-place, its own ballast and weight, its own self-determined glory. Cut off from God, this is a relentless pursuit of self-justification in which other human beings—as value-conferring agents—play a necessary and determinative role, individual identity being ineluctably dialectical, dialogical, or social (cf. Hegel's master/slave relationship). Being fundamentally insecure, we need others to confirm us, to reinforce our identities, to prop up our egos, and so we incline to surround ourselves with self-confirming selves—those just like us. At the very same time, being

---

[27] Reinhold Niebuhr, *The Nature and Destiny of Man*, vol. 1 (New York: Charles Scribner's Sons, 1964). For the following, see esp. 178-86.
[28] In existentialist fashion, anxiety (*Angst*) is to be distinguished here from fear.
[29] Niebuhr, *Nature and Destiny*, 182.
[30] Ibid., 180.
[31] Notes Niebuhr: "That is why Christian orthodoxy has consistently defined unbelief as the root of sin, or as the sin which precedes pride." Ibid., 183.
[32] Ibid., 178.
[33] Ibid., 180
[34] See Bonhoeffer's incisive treatment of original sin as the knowledge of good and evil in *Creation and Fall*, trans. John C. Fletcher (New York: Collier Books, 1959), esp. 64-76.

fundamentally insecure, we also tend to overcompensate in ego support by pridefully establishing ourselves against others. And so we, and like selves, as the extension of ourselves—be it our race, clan, tribe, class, nation, culture, or whatever possessive denomination clung to—we declare our distinction and superiority over others. Self-justification—our primal sin—always seems to entail a surrounding of ourselves by our like selves. Our grasping after equality with God is in every way a grasping of ourselves at the expense and exclusion of others. Listen again to Niebuhr as he captures this dual-aspect of original sin: "The religious dimension of sin is man's rebellion against God, his effort to usurp the place of God. The moral and social dimension of sin is injustice. The ego which falsely makes itself the centre of existence in its pride and will-to-power inevitably subordinates other life to its will and thus does injustice to other life."[35] "All human life," states Niebuhr, "is involved in the sin of seeking security at the expense of other life."[36]

Now the determinants and dynamics of prejudice and racial prejudice, the chief obstacle to the recognition of other groups (i.e., multicultural sensitivity and respect), are many, varied, and complex, and will not detain us. It needs simply to be noted that almost all the literature on prejudice and racism makes reference to insecurity, anxiety, and fear as basic psychological determinants, and to various neurotic compensatory behaviors that attempt to alleviate them.[37] Even if this process of self-justification, self-deification, or self-love, which lies at the base of all interpersonal friction, is, in respect to racial prejudice, elusive to social-scientific quantification or "objective attitude measurement," it appears nonetheless a common observation of human life, Christian or not. Take Freud, for example, who says: "In the undisguised antipathies and aversion which people feel toward strangers with whom they have to do, we recognize the expression of self-love, of narcissism."[38] Or historian Arnold Toynbee, who states:

---

[35] Niebuhr, *Nature and Destiny*, 179.
[36] Ibid., 182.
[37] Note the comment by Selma G. Hirsh in *The Fears Men Live By* (New York: Harper & Brothers, 1955), a book intended as a popular summary of the current state of social scientific studies of prejudice: "The title is accurate. The central thesis of this book is that people are prejudiced because they are afraid. They use their prejudices to conceal their fears" (xi). Further: "Throughout all of the Studies the evidence was indisputable: by the sum of their responses, prejudiced individuals proclaimed their boundless fear." (xvii-xviii; see also 30-32). Cf. also Gordon W. Allport, *The Nature of Prejudice* (Cambridge, Mass.: Addison-Wesley, 1954), a long respected work on this subject, esp. 367ff., which begins with this keynote quote by Jean Paul Sartre: "We are now in a position to understand the anti-Semite. He is a man who is afraid. Not of the Jews, to be sure, but of himself, of his own consciousness, of his liberty, of his instincts, of his responsibilities, of solitariness, of change, of society, and of the world—of everything except the Jews" (367).
[38] Quoted in Kyle Haselden, *The Racial Problem in Christian Perspective* (New York: Harper & Brothers, Publishers, 1959), 76.

every living creature is striving to make itself into a centre of the Universe, and, in the act, is entering into rivalry with every other living creature.... Self-centredness is an intellectual error because no living creature is in truth the centre of the Universe; and it is also a moral error, because no living creature has a right to act as if he were the centre of the Universe.[39]

Kyle Haselden puts it well by way of summary: "viewed historically, racial prejudice ... is not really a new thing but simply the latest and most virulent form of man's ancient urge for self-exaltation ... put theologically, [it] is one of man's several neurotic and perverted expressions of his will to be God."[40]

This is not to say that each and every one of us expresses our prejudice or "acts it out" in a gradient range of neurotic behavior,[41] but like the plague of original sin, and reflective of it, it is in us all, and its infectious spread casts its tentacles long and wide. If we take an honest look, we will see it within, and we will see it without. If we claim immunity here, we deceive ourselves and the truth is not in us. Racial prejudice and its objectified forms can be overt or covert; intentional or unintentional; individual, institutional, or cultural. As Benjamin Buford Blue, a.k.a. "Bubba," Forrest Gump's ebonic alter-ego might put it: "You can barbecue it, boil it, broil it, bake it, sauté it, deep-, pan- or stir-fry it ... and that ain't about all." In the prejudice "biness" there is a myriad of ways of serving up this commodity. While many of us in the majority culture may be well-intentioned people of Christian virtue who *have* taken a long and hard look inside ourselves, we can nonetheless at the same time be unintentional and covert transmitters of the institutional and cultural racisms of the society in which we live, principalities and powers from which we may derive benefit.

Do nothing out of selfish ambition or vain conceit, says Paul, but in humility consider others better than yourselves—namely by looking also to their interests and welfare (Phil. 2:3-4). It is interesting to note that the Greek word for "vain conceit" (2:3), which can also be a synonym for "selfish [or excessive] ambition," is *kenodoxia*—literally, empty glory. *Kenodoxia* has secondary meanings of "illusion," "delusion," or "error."[42] The glory that the first Adam sought above and beyond the God-given glory he already had was an "empty glory," a "vainglory," since it was sought out of his own ambition and conceit. I have argued that one way of talking about original sin is to view it as self-justification, and that one fundamental way we justify ourselves is

---

[39]Quoted in Ibid., 76-77.
[40]Ibid., 82, 84.
[41]For example, frustration-aggression, scapegoating, stereotyping, frustration-tolerance, projection of undesirable traits, mental rigidity, authoritarian personality, and the like.
[42]Walter Bauer, *A Greek-English Lexicon of the New Testament and Other Early Christian Literature*, trans. and adapt. William F. Arndt and F. Wilbur Gingrich, 4th ed. (Chicago: University of Chicago Press, 1957), 428.

by confirming our lives with like others in anywhere from subtle to malicious devaluation of unlike others. This also is an empty glory. And indeed, to the degree we selfishly ensconce ourselves in safe and self-confirming surroundings, such security, like *kenodoxia* in its secondary sense, is an "illusion," "delusion," and "error." Our proud wardrobes of resemblance—in which we merely mirror and confirm one another in suits of similarity and leathers of likeness—may very well prove to be our fig leaves of shame, and such attire won't finally hide us from the face of God.

But that very face has again appeared to us in tempered guise, in the self-effacing life of Christ. His venture into the far country (Barth) of human history is, according to Philippians 2, a reaching out by one society of persons for the welfare of an other—God the Trinity for us. Our docetic perspectives on Christ prevent us from fully appreciating the length of this reach. But the Incarnation of the Son of God was no walk in the park. The one who was rich in divine glory became poor for our sakes (2 Cor. 8:9a); though he was in the form of God, he emptied himself and became human. Without regard to his status and security he risked his identity in the interests of an other; he emptied himself of something rightly his, that in his poverty we might become rich (2 Cor. 8:9b).

Now if the second Adam for the welfare of an other crossed the great metaphysical divide between God and humanity, Creator and creature, can we not in imitation of him cross the less-essential divides that separate us, to encounter and embrace those who are also created in the very same image? It is, finally, not that much of a stretch: from one human person to the next, from one image-bearer to another. But like Madison Avenue, it does seem to be all about image. If we in the Christian church are ungraceful about affirming others because we stumble over distinctions of race, ethnicity, or culture, then it is quite possible that we have too tight of a grip on our own lives, a false (i.e., insecure) image of ourselves, which we may have to learn to ungrasp.

"Your attitude should be the same as that of Christ Jesus," says the apostle Paul (Phil. 2:5). In imitation of Christ we are called to empty ourselves. But unlike that One who emptied himself of an all-entitled glory, we must empty ourselves of an unentitled one, a stolen one, one that, finally, is but a *kenodoxia*, a vain and empty glory. This is not much of a loss. Paul says as much a chapter later where he easily considers his legal Jewish pedigree a loss compared to the surpassing greatness of knowing Christ and attaining to his righteousness (Phil. 3:5-9).

But ungrasping ourselves is a painful process because it involves a risk, a risk of identity. Yet, this also, finally, is not much of a risk. Like the Pascalian wager, the odds are unbeatable. Jesus puts them this way: "If you cling to your life, you will lose it; but if you give it up for Me, you will save it."[43] For an insecure humanity, this seems to be an offer we cannot refuse. And I take it

---

[43]Matt. 10:39, Living New Testament.

that this principle applies not only to individuals, but to corporate bodies and personalities and institutions of the Christian church as well. Like the One who humbled himself and risked his identity in dependence upon God, only to be exalted, we also must commit our lives, our identities, to God, that in Christ we may come to our true selves. "To be in Christ is to be reconciled with one another as a community of racially and ethnically diverse people of God," states the Christian Reformed Church's Synodical Report.[44] To the degree that this is not evident in our corporate life, to the degree that we are not willing that this be evident, is the degree to which we are still grasping ourselves and in need of a modification of identity, a kenotic makeover. This risk of identity, however, is nothing other than the Christian venture of faith, a challenge that should be eagerly met by any tradition whose heartfelt motto is *semper reformanda*—always reforming.

---

[44]"God's Diverse and Unified Family," 8.

Widening the Emptying: A Response to Thomas R. Thompson

Leanne Van Dyk

THOMAS R. THOMPSON PROPOSES a kenotic model of multicultural encounter. This model incorporates a number of themes, including an analysis of the primal sin of human beings, the classic Adam-Christ typology, and a call for *imitatio Christi* patterned on the kenosis hymn of Philippians 2.

My general response to Professor Thompson's essay is wholeheartedly affirmative. I found his exegesis and theological analysis perceptive and convincing. This is the kind of theological reflection much needed in both the academy and the church today: reflection that is well integrated with the witness of Scripture and the resources of the broad sweep of systematic theology.

However, I suggest that the kenotic model of multicultural encounter that Thompson explicates be expanded. This is because the kenotic model, based as it is on an analysis of human self-justification, human self-definition, and *kenodoxia*—vain conceit or empty glory—is a model that is only *partially descriptive* of human beings. That is to say, Reinhold Niebuhr's theory that sin at its root is an inordinate will-to-power—a construct that Professor Thompson employs in his model—does not account for all human experience.

Almost forty years ago, Valerie Saiving Goldstein wrote an important article that is now a small classic of a very early and remarkably tentative feminist theology.[1] The article, whose insights were taken up in book form by Judith Plaskow, suggests that Niebuhr's analysis of sin is only valid for dominant people or peoples.[2] That is, only people with power express their fundamental anxiety and finitude with an inordinate will-to-power. Only people used to directing and controlling other people can even presume that they direct and control their own destiny.

Women, Saiving Goldstein pointed out, do not express their fundamental anxiety and finitude by these sorts of sins; rather, they experience sin in quite a different way: "It is my contention that there are significant differences between masculine and feminine experience and that feminine experience reveals in a more emphatic fashion certain aspects of the human situation which are present but less obvious in the experience of men."[3] Saiving Goldstein's critique of Niebuhr and much of the classic Christian tradition, although perhaps overly "essentialist," nonetheless conveys a fundamental feminist insight—namely, that women's experience is different from men's

---

[1] Valerie Saiving Goldstein, "The Human Situation: A Feminine View," *Journal of Religion* 40 (April 1960), 100-112.
[2] Judith Plaskow, *Sex, Sin, and Grace; Women's Experience and the Theologies of Reinhold Niebuhr and Paul Tillich* (Washington: University Press of America, 1980).
[3] Saiving Goldstein, "The Human Situation," 101.

experience.[4] The theological importance of this basic insight in the context of this response to Thompson is that women's sin is different from men's sin. Thus, the spiritual discipline required to overcome women's sin will be different from the spiritual discipline required to overcome men's sin.

For Saiving Goldstein, and Plaskow in her expansion of the thesis, women's sin is much more likely to be that of self-negation, passivity, and false dependence. Plaskow identifies this sin as "the failure to take responsibility for self-actualization," and Saiving Goldstein calls it the "undevelopment or negation of the self."[5] If this feminist insight is correct, then a kenotic model of multicultural encounter does not seem to fit women's experience or that of other peoples who have been marginalized or oppressed.[6] Such people may have no empty glory or pride to kenotically give up in order to make room for the other. A different—or at least modified—model of multicultural encounter is needed for peoples who have experienced a decided lack of power and thus possess little pride to tempt them to empty glory.

The foundation of the modified model is still *imitatio Christi*, but the strategies toward imitation of Christ are diverse. For dominant people, a kenosis of power and privilege is the challenge—those who traditionally hold power, those who are so used to power that to think of a world in which that power is shared is deeply threatening. For these people, a kenosis of self-glorification is the way to *imitatio Christi*.

For subjugated people, for those whose historical and traditional role has been secondary, derivative, even one of oppression, there is a different sort of giving up, a different sort of kenosis. For these people—women, the poor, the socially disadvantaged, racial and ethnic minorities—a kenosis of self-negation is the way to *imitatio Christi*.

For these peoples, these voices and faces in a multicultural encounter, the key text will not be Philippians 2:6-7. The key text may be 1 Peter 2:10: "Once you were no people, but now you are God's people; once you had not received mercy, but now you have received mercy." This text presents a kenosis of a different sort—a kenosis of no name into a new identity of name, a kenosis of no personhood into a new pride of personhood.

---

[4]Saiving Goldstein was aware, as are feminist thinkers today, that the claim that women's experience is different from men's experience must not be overinterpreted. That is, gender is a social construction and thus highly flexible and diverse, depending on the cultural context.

[5]Plaskow, *Sex, Sin, and Grace*, 3; Saiving Goldstein, "The Human Situation," 108.

[6]The words "oppressed women's experience" have become problematic for many feminist thinkers in recent years. The experiences of sexism that a middle-class white woman experiences are different from the experiences of sexism combined with racism that an African American woman experiences. Thus, overly generalizing women's oppression is not helpful in feminist thought and is sometimes considered patronizing by racial-ethnic women. Yet, some modest generalization is necessary for the purpose of this essay.

I am suggesting that the kenotic model of multicultural encounter that Thompson has articulated is fitting for people used to having power but not for people who have been rendered powerless by a dominant culture. I am also suggesting that the kenotic pattern can be expanded so as to be appropriate to traditionally excluded peoples. The difference is the type of kenosis required. For the dominant groups, a kenosis of a will-to-power and self-glorification is required—in short, a kenosis of pride. For the marginalized, a kenosis of having no name is required—an emptying out of self-hatred, passivity, and false dependence.

The benefit of this expanded model, one that accounts for several sorts of kenotic emptying, is not only in its clearer diagnostic ability. Not only does an expanded model account for the diverse experiences of men and women, powerful and oppressed, racially dominant and racially marginalized; it also gives a richer account of God's grace in particular human lives. Judith Plaskow remarks that in her effort to analyze and articulate women's experience, she noticed that "sin may flourish and grace abound where they have not yet been suspected."[7] A perhaps unexpected benefit of taking all human experience into account in theological reflection is that God's gracious resolve and ingenuity is highlighted. Small epiphanies of the particularity of God's grace that nonetheless has cosmic significance are revealed.

If dominant groups can find a path toward multicultural encounter in a kenosis of kenodoxia, and if repressed groups can find their path toward multicultural encounter in a true discovery of self, a mutual identity must be found together in Christ. The rush for claiming difference and particularly that characterizes many multicultural discussions must not, in Christian circles, eclipse a common identity in Jesus Christ. Given that many seminaries—and some Christian colleges as well—are deeply divided along racial, ideological, and gender lines, I am convinced that an unending narrative of difference is not ultimately helpful. Individual stories, as important as they are, find their true place in *the* Story, the story that the Scriptures narrate, the story of God's grand plan of action for humanity in Jesus Christ. This story has the power and promise to shape us, identify us, and unite us more than all our individual narratives. The Christian community, in all its wonderful diversity and difference, must reclaim unity by professing faith in and commitment to the story of Jesus Christ.

---

[7]Plaskow, *Sex, Sin, and Grace*, 175.

Racial Reconciliation in South Africa and the Theological Winds of Change That Inspired It

Caesar Molebatsi

THE DISCUSSION ABOUT racial reconciliation in South Africa always presents us with a very difficult case because the nature of the inhumanity perpetrated in South Africa falls so unevenly along racial lines. At the same time, the responsibility to promote racial harmony falls more heavily upon the victims of this inhumanity than it does on its perpetrators. This has serious and wide-ranging implications for South Africa, even for its national budget, for example, which must take into account the enormous cost and debt that the new, fledgling government will have to bear in the interest in reparations. We in South Africa, therefore, do not discuss this subject lightly, for already the writing is on the wall in terms of cost. But while this cost can be spelled out in financial terms, it is even more so to be reckoned in emotional terms as victims are asked to forgive and overcome personal pain and suffering. In this regard, Mandela's leadership is exemplary and falls nothing short of miraculous.

Initially, around the mid-1980s, any talk of reconciliation to the millions of South Africans who were victims of apartheid suggested capitulation, betrayal, cover-up of past injustices, denial of our history, and negation of our culture. This was the case until the work of the Truth and Reconciliation Commission (hereafter TRC) spelled out what it would take to have true reconciliation in the country. Any idea of a soft, happy-clappy, bind-us-together sort of reconciliation was totally obliterated by the public deliberations of the TRC. The TRC moved the discussion of reconciliation away from the comfort zone of liberal theoretical discourse to the concrete personal and historical reality of a suffering people. Here we were being brutally confronted on a daily basis with the bare evil and unrelenting devastation of apartheid. The extent of pain inflicted on ordinary South Africans was revealed to be of such a magnitude that its continual exposure in the public media threatened the very possibility of reconciliation. This outrage and cry for justice in South Africa forced the Christian community to look soberly at the demands of racial reconciliation.

In this essay I will sketch a brief narrative of the developments within the Christian church of South Africa which led it to its present and key role in postapartheid racial reconciliation, a key role given that 77 percent of South Africans profess some version of Christianity. Along the way of this checkered narrative, I will identify the major theological themes that emerged from church debate and that underpin the present attitudes toward racial reconciliation, making it both a real possibility and an increasing reality in South Africa today.

Developments Within the Church

It is undeniable that the church played a very crucial role leading up to the establishment of democracy in South Africa. But the road of that involvement was neither smooth nor straight. While the church's participation in national politics was ultimately guided by its own inner theological rationale, it was also influenced along the way by factors external to itself—by the political strategies of both the liberation movements and the South African apartheid government.

Such political involvement can first be detected in the fifties when the government vigorously began implementing laws relating to education. The liberal church in particular was catapulted into action when the government of South Africa closed the mission schools in 1954. This forced the complacent gentlemen within the landed gentry (which the established church had become in South Africa) to realize that *even they* were not safe from the evil tentacles of the apartheid legislation that was enacted in 1948. Please bear in mind that our theme, racial reconciliation and the theological winds that inspired it, has much to do with the motif of "justice and jubilee," a biblical foundation for change that bears a very direct relationship to issues of land and its distribution. The establishment church to this day still owns vast amounts of land acquired under the guise of setting up mission stations for the African population. The offense it took at the governmental action of 1954 is a clear case of mixed motivation.

The decisive moment when the church received her wake–up call, however, was in 1960 at the Cottesloe Conference, when the Dutch Reformed Church (DRC), which many dubbed "the National Party government at prayer," walked out in anger. The international church community was demanding that they distance themselves from the government's policy of separate development—apartheid—a policy for which the church to that point had afforded theological justification. The DRC dismissed the international church leadership with contempt, asserting that it is inappropriate to mix religion with politics.

This brought about a split in the church community in South Africa. By walking out of the Cottesloe Conference, the DRC disassociated itself from the South African Council of Churches (SACC). As a result, members of the DRC who were progressive in their politics were forced to take a stance against their own church. People such as Dr. Beyers Naudé had to set up alternative structures, such as the Christian Institute. This organization became the main platform for those who were seen as dissidents of the DRC. Their main activity was to publicize an alternative theological reflection that took into consideration the suffering of the vast majority of South Africans. Such activity served to conscientize the white community, and at the same time gave black theologians hope that change could be influenced by applying the biblical principles regarding the kingdom of God. This was an important development, for if this had not happened, any prospects for racial reconciliation in the future would lose the black leadership that it would desperately need.

It is important to note that at this time the mainline evangelical church was not engaged in any serious theological reflection in dialogue with the unfolding political and social situation. This was the case because most of its theological education was dominated by the expatriate missionary establishment that had bound itself to a position of noninvolvement in the political matters of the nation that was hosting them. Inasmuch as this was understandable, it fed into the conservative mindset of the DRC, which held that you do not mix your religion with politics. But this development caused black evangelicals to lose the opportunity to be involved in their community in a manner that would give them credibility and integrity. As a result, black evangelicals became known for being subacademic as well as subeconomic, and accordingly not to be taken seriously. Black evangelicals with an activist bent were, more often than not, forced to abandon their own fellowships to be able to participate in issues of political and social transformation.

The split within the church was beginning to develop along four basic lines.

The DRC Family of Churches. This became a very important arena of the national struggle since there were those who did not leave the DRC family but who continued to voice their dissent from within. Such people were often very severely restricted, a restricting done with the collaboration of the DRC and the government. This can be seen, for example, in the sidelining, house arrest, and banning of Dr. Naudé, an ordeal that lasted for more than a decade.

Some DRC colored and black clergy maintained a relationship with the South African Council of Churches (SACC) and its varied structures around the country, and some like Dr. Allan Boesak promoted a strong political agenda that was linked to the international movement of the Reformed churches. This linkage led to the famous denunciation of apartheid as a heresy at the Vancouver meeting of the World Reform Movement in the late eighties.

The SACC Family. This grouping of churches maintained a very strong political stance and became the training ground for many of the future political leaders of the country, including Dr. Frank Chikane, currently the Director General in the Office of the Deputy President, and expected to assume the presidency after Mandela in 1999; Sakie Macozoma, who initially headed up the communications department for the new government and is now the head of the second largest parastatal which includes South African Airways; Joe Seremanc, who currently heads up the Land Claims Commission; and many others who assumed the basic leadership at the administrative level for the new government that came to power in 1994.

The theological perspective of SACC was greatly influenced by the reflections of leaders such as Cedric Mason, who believed that "Jesus meant what he said about the Kingdom of God on earth. The context of Christianity is not heaven but earth."[1] Accordingly, SACC involvement was driven by a praxis-oriented theology. It went on to play a significant role in intervening on behalf of political prisoners and trialists and became the main conduit of assistance for families whose members were victimized by the apartheid regime.

The Independent Churches. These churches were by far the largest in terms of membership. They are the indigenous churches that sought to contextualize the Christian faith in line with African traditions. Since these groups were apolitical, they were wooed at different times by various political leaders. Their significance was seen only to the extent that they could influence the vote at the polls when a new dispensation was being called for. Only when the Union Movement became strong in South Africa did it become important for these churches to be considered as allies by the mass democratic movement. Unlike SACC, their involvement was not significantly motivated by any theological reflection.

The Evangelical Church. Evangelicalism as practiced within South Africa was viewed as a conservative movement. That equation was unfortunate because for many people, theological conservatism was expected to go hand in hand with political conservatism, which in the South African context meant acquiescence to the status quo. Those more politically active had to seek fellowship and support elsewhere, which is essentially what happened to individuals such as Cyril Ramaphose, who was chair of the Constitutional Assembly that produced the present constitution of South Africa, as well as Khehla Mtembu, Lybo Mabaso, and others who founded the Azanian People's Movement (AZAPO).

What happened within the DRC family was replicated within the evangelical movement in that many in this community also began to seek a new ecclesial identity, one that included an active engagement of racial issues. Consequently, many evangelicals embarked on a serious theological study of social issues, inspired especially by the reflections of the English evangelical social reformers of the eighteenth century, such as Wilberforce and Lord Shaftesbury, and of evangelists such as the Wesley brothers.

The black evangelical church soon came to realize that their lack of socially engaged theology was largely due to their origin in foreign missions, an evangelical enterprise that did not so much as prize contextual theological reflection.

It is widely acknowledged today that South African liberation movements, especially the African National Congress (ANC) deliberately sought to engage the church as an important ally in the national struggle. The division within the church was clearly understood by movement leaders, and out of this understanding came a calculated strategy to influence and to harness its moral and suasive powers for the purpose of speeding up the

---

[1]Quoted in Rachel Tingle, *Revolution or Reconciliation?: The Struggle in the Church in South Africa* (London: Christian Studies Centre, 1992), 137.

demise of the apartheid regime. For example, an article appearing in *The African Communist* stated that

> in our country, the majority of those who will participate in the final overthrow of the apartheid colonial regime are church goers. Neglect of this factor . . . may reduce the effectiveness of our vanguard role among the masses, and lose us sections of the potential fighting force. . . . Having realized that the majority of the working masses in our country are Christians, revolutionaries should then look for ways and means of involving the Church in the national liberation struggle in general and the working-class struggle in particular.[2]

This deliberate targeting and mobilizing of the church toward the struggle became an official position of the ANC. Among other things, the 1985 Kabwe Consultative Conference recommended the following:

> The Movement (i.e., the ANC) recognizes the fact that a large portion of our people are religious or come from particular religious backgrounds. . . . By raising the political consciousness of this community, influencing them to accept the politics of the Movement, especially the Freedom Charter, and a commitment to the creation of a non-racial, democratic South Africa, all should strive to convert them into centers of resistance and struggle.[3]

The ANC so recognized the importance and potential of the church's theological deliberations that they even made this recommendation: "We should aim to create ANC units both within the established churches and independent churches and other religious bodies."[4] Even more particularly: "The Movement should give attention to the institutions like the Institute of Contextual Theology. We should aim at giving political content and direction to the work."[5]

It is interesting to note that not too long after this recommendation, the Institute of Contextual Theology produced the Kairos Document that enjoins the church to be active on all levels in the national struggle and upon whose publication ANC President Oliver Tambo, himself a Methodist churchman, declared on Radio Freedom: "This document, fellow countrymen, could not

---

[2] Thoko Mdialose, *The African Communist*, (First Quarter, 1986), quoted in Tingle, *Revolution or Reconciliation?* 136.
[3] "Commission on Cadre Policy, Political and Ideological Work," ANC Internal Report on the Second National Consultative Conference in Kabwe, Zambia, 2-6 July 1985, 10, quoted in Tingle, *Revolution or Reconciliation?* 138.
[4] Ibid., 139.
[5] Ibid.

have come at any better time than now. . . . Gone are the days when our people understood Christianity to mean neutrality and passivity in politics."[6]

While the influence of liberation movements was a definite factor in motivating and mobilizing the church toward the national struggle, the greater influence came from the church's own inner rationale, the theology of which also set it up to play the key role in postapartheid racial reconciliation. To that checkered narrative we now turn.

Racial Reconciliation: Winds of Change That Inspired It, Theological Underpinnings.

The theological underpinnings of the present attitudes toward reconciliation in South Africa can be traced in several ways. One way is to look at the various movements and their manifestos during this period of struggle. Another way is to examine the variety of books and documents that have been produced during this time. I will proceed mostly by way of the former and conclude by recommending two of the latter.

Many prominent ecclesiastical movements to emerge since the mid-seventies can be traced to the different crises that were experienced by the South African people and that would call for the church to respond. There were eight such movements.

South African Christian Leadership Assembly (SACLA). The SACLA was organized by church leaders who were concerned that the deteriorating situation in the country demanded a response from the church. Their intention was to showcase the possibility of reconciliation in the context of apartheid by witnessing to a faith in Christ that overcomes the artificial barriers set up by human beings. Here church leaders met and publicly displayed their fellowship despite their various racial and ecclesiastical backgrounds. The SACLA was a major breakthrough for the South African church since it cut across deep denominational divides.

More particularly, an important bridge was built between the theological divide that had developed since Cottesloe. For the first time, black evangelicals were able to meet their counterparts in the so-called liberal church and find camaraderie. Consequently, a new way of doing theology surfaced, and new avenues of cooperation were established. This dramatically changed the theological landscape because serious theological work was now to be guided also by contextual considerations rather than by theological tradition alone. Theology became something that could be done—a "doing theology"—as opposed to something simply transmitted. South-to-South dialogue also became an important activity, as Latin American experiences were taken into account in our reflections to help us understand God and His good agenda for South Africa.

---

[6]Radio Freedom, 3 October 1985, quoted in Tingle, *Revolution or Reconciliation*, 141.

The Institute of Contextual Theology (ICT). The ICT introduced a hermeneutic of suspicion. It engaged in a re-reading of Scripture from the perspective of the underclass. The ICT encouraged a theological reflection that was more consciously sensitive to context, and they published literature and promoted conferences that embraced a wider spread of traditions. Here various groups—Catholics who did not belong to the SACC, evangelicals who had no means of publishing, even the liberal church—were able to meet and discuss issues of mutual concern.

Out of the ICT came one of the most outstanding documents to generate debate among the South African church: the Kairos Document. This document was intended to be a clarion call for the church to carry out its responsibility to critique the prevailing theology that undergirded, either directly or indirectly, the state regime and its rationalization of abusive power. The language and subject matter of the Kairos Document made it impossible for anyone to disregard its challenge.

Evangelical Fellowship of South Africa (EFSA). The EFSA was established in the tradition of the World Evangelical Fellowship with expatriate leadership and multinational organizational support, and was intended in the main to stem the tide of liberalism. Though it sought to perpetuate the traditional missionary approach to the problems of the community, it was later to be significantly influenced toward a more sociopolitical sensitivity.

The National Initiative for Reconciliation (NIR). This movement was a direct result of the momentum that was built up at the SACLA conference. The NIR was to become one of the main forces to promote the idea of racial reconciliation in South Africa. The efforts of this movement centered on justice, and for the first time, the business community became involved in the reconciliation debate. It is especially interesting to note that as the nature of justice was thoroughly explored, the biblical principles of jubilee were openly broached.

This quest to understand justice drove many to embrace the biblical idea of jubilee. Given the extent of dispossession, dehumanization, and denial of human rights and freedoms in South Africa, any idea of justice was for many South Africans a mere pipe dream, something so idealistic that it could not be achieved. But the thinking here was that it is not possible to talk about justice without considering issues of restitution because justice by its very nature demands the redressing of past injustice. Any just settlement in South Africa, however, could lead to a major upheaval because the extensive cost of restitution could destroy the economic infrastructure—the very one developed at the expense of the majority of South Africans through their dispossession of land and opportunity. The implications for reconstruction were very serious, if not a potential nightmare. The jubilee demands for justice as understood in both the Old and New Testaments caused vigorous discussion and debate.

Koinonia. While the NIR was admired for its deliberations, many felt that it and other groups were not doing well enough in turning theological theory into practice. It was the tremendous vision of Dr. Nico Smith to try to change this by establishing the movement of Koinonia. Its primary aim was to incarnate the message of reconciliation by pairing individual families from different racial backgrounds to experience and participate in each other's life and culture. Here individuals as well as groups were afforded various settings where they could encounter the diverse others around them.

But these efforts were seen by many as too little, too late, lacking the necessary political punch of the more visible demonstrations against the government, as afforded by marches and boycotts, which had become characteristic of the more militant organizations.

Concerned Evangelicals (CE). Concerned evangelicals was born out of the desire to deal effectively with issues of violence as well as to minister to the victims of the state regime. Until its formation, a dualist theology that did not take the interrelatedness of the sacred and secular into account had resulted in an evangelical paralysis in the face of the state's relentlessly violent response to the black community's demand for democracy. The initial concern of CE was to remove the "log" in our own eye—that is black evangelical acquiescence to the theological domination of the West—before attempting to remove the "speck" from the eyes of those who had brought this dualistic theology.

It is essential to understand that contextual considerations drove this group in its theological reflections, as is poignantly portrayed in the preface of its important manifesto *Evangelical Witness in South Africa* (EWISA):

> Whilst this group of concerned evangelicals was meeting in one of the churches in Orlando, Soweto, the security forces stormed into the school next to the church and kids were seen breaking window-panes and escaping through the windows. . . . Some children were arrested. . . . The group felt helpless . . . Then came the second scene when the school kids became angry about what the security forces did. . . . They stoned a commercial vehicle, stopped it, let the driver go and attempted to put it on fire. As this second scene occurred we agonized about our role in this situation. If we failed to intervene in the legalized brutal violence of the security forces what right do we have to intervene in the counter-violence of the kids? On the other hand the African National Congress (ANC) had called for a people's war in 1986 to defend people against the security forces of apartheid South Africa which they said were killing defenseless people in the townships. What was our response supposed to be in this situation as evangelical Christians in South Africa?[7]

---

[7]Concerned Evangelicals, *Evangelical Witness in South Africa: A Critique of*

Given this context, black evangelicals could not simply execute their usual programs of evangelism and church planting. The black evangelical entered the struggle for liberation.

CE, however, was caught in the dilemma of being able to relate meaningfully to other groups, such as the SACC, while holding on to a strong evangelical agenda, an agenda that had become difficult to represent because of the lack of credibility this community suffered by virtue of *white evangelical* compliance with the apartheid laws.

CE began with a series of meetings, discussion groups, workshops, and seminars, firstly around Soweto. Out of these meetings came a draft of concerns (April 1986), which was then circulated around the country for further consultation. Often, such discussion would be kicked off by asking a series of simple questions, such as, "What is the Lord doing or saying in your life at this time?" Scripture would also be explored to test the validity of our conclusions. After many debates and symposiums, the issues boiled down to one: the basis for the demands of justice.

To the basic question, "What are the demands of justice?" came the rationale, indeed slogan, that "there is no peace without justice, hence if you want peace work for justice. There is no justice without restitution, therefore, if you want justice you must fight for the people's claim for restitution." But it was clear, especially to believers, that restitution by its very nature could inflict a serious crack in the fragile peace that existed between races and ethnic groups. It was determined, therefore, after a careful study of the Scriptures, that to demand justice and restitution also required believers-as-victims to offer a heavy dose of mercy. This was biblically rooted in the idea that God loved justice and righteousness as tempered by mercy.

It is noteworthy that the black community at this time did not differentiate between charismatic and noncharismatic believers, as did the white community. Charismatic leaders in the while suburbs were not entirely pleased by this and a powerful group was formed in the attempt to perpetuate an exclusively charismatic fellowship among black churches. But the latter generally banded together under the rubric of evangelical.

It is also interesting to note that the term progressive evangelical began to be used to identify those who embraced a more holistic Gospel, a Gospel understood as the power of God that brings a salvation that transforms persons *and their environments*. For the first time in the history of the evangelical church in South Africa (dating back at least to 1948) there was a recognition that evil can be systemic and mediated by structures, be they political, economic, or even religious ones—structures themselves that must become objects of salvation, or in the popular parlance, transformation.

Concerned Evangelicals considered themselves an interim group whose purpose was to catalyze the formation of a truly representative evangelical

---

Evangelical Theology and Practice by South African Evangelicals (Grand Rapids: Eerdmans, 1986), 17.

voice in South Africa, one with credibility and one that could be involved in ecumenical issues on a wide scale.

International Fellowship of Charismatic Churches (IFCC). The IFCC formed to stem the tide of a perceived impotence of charismatic Christianity to deal with the reality of suffering in South Africa. While the mainline churches had tapped the theological resources of the Cross for their engagement of social ills and demand for public repentance, the charismatics were largely viewed as promoting a private, pietistic faith, one exclusively concerned with the individual's economic and physical security and spiritual affirmation. To alter this image, the IFCC became involved in a variety of social services to help alleviate human suffering, all the while being careful not to engage in any teaching or practice that could be viewed as challenging the structural evil of apartheid. Much of the affluent community of South Africa were members of this group of churches.

The Evangelical Alliance of South Africa (TEASA). As a result of the ongoing concern of evangelicals with a strong social conscience, located within the various movements discussed thus far, the time had come for a new evangelical formation. Fortunately, as Concerned Evangelicals began discussions about evangelical unity, groups such as the NIR and SACLA, along with individuals such as Michael Cassidy and Ray MacCauley saw the need to unite. CE was able, as the most vocal black evangelical group, to rally these forces around and under the leadership of General Secretary Moss Nthlha, and formed TEASA. It is a fledgling movement that is still struggling to clearly establish its identity.

We can identify three important commonalties of these various movements that have enabled them to work together for racial reconciliation and the healing of the nation. First, we have *a new hermeneutic*. In the process of rereading Scripture from the "underside," the notion of *historical context* took on a new meaning for us. Evangelicals and liberals alike recognized the need to take account of the ancient context of the biblical writers as well as the contemporary context of the interpreter of Scripture in applying its truths. This was, and still is, a disconcerting development for many Western theologians and biblical scholars, but it gave to the South African Christian community a way to deal with sensitive biblical texts such as Romans 12, Acts 4, the book of Philemon, as well as other misappropriated Pauline texts.

Second, we have *the quest for unity and embracing of the reconstruction agenda*. It is widely acknowledged today that the church community has to play a pivotal role in assisting our nation to walk back into its history to expose the truth, and to do this in such a way that a firm foundation is laid for the healing of the nation. This includes a deliberate attempt to assist victims in regaining some sense of dignity and material well being, while affording the perpetrators of violence the experience of forgiveness and catharsis by giving them an opportunity to "come clean." This process is also being carried out publicly by the Truth and Reconciliation Commission under the leadership of Archbishop Desmond Tutu.

Third, we have *public confession*. It became increasingly clear that what South Africa needed was not only a single voice coming from the Christian community, but a public demonstration of that unity—including both a visible repentance and challenge of the status quo. The Rustenburg Conference in 1991 was a major breakthrough in this respect since it stretched "from Catholic to Calvinist to Charismatic" with the important consequence that "the failures of the churches . . . in allowing and even condoning the development of the serious social ills that [had] befallen the country over the past years, were acknowledged and confessed."[8] There have been many such events since, including: the FNB Soccer Stadium rally in Soweto, where Bishop Tutu led all the major political leaders, including President Mandela, to kneel publicly before the cross, thereby acknowledging their dependence upon God; the Ellis Park Stadium rally, involving the amalgamation of the largest charismatic church in South Africa, and including Rev. Dr. Frank Chikane, founder-member of Concerned Evangelicals and the then leader of the Apostolic Faith Mission Church (Pentecostal); and the recent pilgrimage to Robben Island, where an acknowledgment of the atrocities of the past and a commitment to racial reconciliation by church leaders was nationally televised.

It is of paramount importance for me to mention that one of the main factors driving this unified reflection and activity was the intensity and nature of the theological debate that raged over the past two decades. Such debate occurred out of a sense of obligation—the need to engage in dialogue with other Christian groups. People participated out of a strong sense of "having to work things out." Dialogue here was no luxury, but was seen to be an important part of what God required for the salvation of the nation. Even though there was an initial resistance to such discussions by the more conservative groups, it became clear by the time of the Rustenburg Conference that even those of a more conservative bent had, in obedience to God, to seek to understand others and in turn be understood.

These debates centered around several themes, especially those of *reconciliation, justice, restitution, witness, peace*, and *transformation*. It was the concern for being credible Christian witnesses that seemed to drive all these theological trends into a mainstream of cooperation and unity, despite their diversity of cultures and theological traditions. Such debate almost always started with a discussion around the plea for reconciliation. A typical response would be that there can be no reconciliation without justice. But biblical justice required restitution (cf. Zaccheus), and restitution required repentance. Being repentant created an atmosphere in which a witness to the Lordship of Christ could take place. Repentance had to be met with a spirit of

---

[8]Louw Alberts and Frank Chikane, *The Road to Rustenburg* (Capetown: Struik Christian Books, 1991), 9.

forgiveness, an essential ingredient for making peace. In the context where peace prevails, transformation becomes possible. This was the typical progression of thinking in these debates.

On a sociopolitical level, both government and civil society could not begin the process of reconstruction and healing until theologians, the church, and society at large—a society in which 77 percent of its people professed Christianity—dealt with these issues in an effective way.

In conclusion, let me recommend two books that well illustrate the theological debate within South Africa. Although there have been many publications this past decade relevant to our topic, these two volumes in particular are of special interest in identifying the theological underpinnings of the present attitudes toward racial reconciliation: Albert Nolan's, *God in South Africa*,[9] and Michael Cassidy's, *The Passing Summer*.[10]

Even though the authors did not envision the split that was to happen among readers, it is fair to say that these two books exemplified, upon their publication, the two main streams of thought within the South African population concerning the matter of racial reconciliation. Cassidy's book largely articulated the white perspective in South Africa—those who, as the title suggested, were fearful that their day in the sun was passing into a winter of discontent, fearful even of black retaliation as the judgment of God.

Nolan's book, however, largely articulated the view of the oppressed majority, those not necessarily evangelical in persuasion, but who nonetheless took the social responsibility of the church seriously. He saw the Bible and read it from the underside. Speaking for those upon whom the apartheid laws had been inflicted, Nolan did not see the future as a winter of discontent; if anything, it was the dawn of a new day, the onset of summer, a future to look forward to rather than one that brought the punishment of God with it.

Inasmuch as Nolan and Cassidy showed the black and white divide on this issue, the Kairos and EWISA documents, already discussed, gave ample evidence that there was enough theological depth and political aptitude in the black community to lead the church in South Africa to a meaningful, effective, and peaceful debate and experience of racial reconciliation, resulting in a powerful witness to the principles of the kingdom of God, a kingdom in which there is neither Jew nor Greek, slave nor free, black nor white. To such an end we in South Africa continue to commit our endeavors.

---

[9]Albert Nolan, *God in South Africa: The Challenge of the Gospel* (Grand Rapids: Eerdmans, 1988).
[10]Michael Cassidy, *The Passing Summer: A South African's Response to White Fear, Black Anger, and the Politics of Love* (Ventura, Calif.: Regal Books/African Enterprise, 1990).

Reformed Theology at Work: A Response to Caesar Molebatsi

Glandion W. Carney[1]

IN 1994, A Nigerian doing postgraduate work at the University of Pretoria said that he had left Christianity. When asked why, he replied, "If these white men who brought Christianity to Africa don't want to share South Africa with us, how do we know they will share heaven with us?"

What is most unfortunate about this statement is not what it says about the church's involvement in creating apartheid; rather, it is that it denies the positive role the church played in fighting and dismantling apartheid. As Caesar Molebatsi teaches us, the church in South Africa did play a big role in that struggle. We hope that history will recognize this and that people will remember the church for its greater role in apartheid's demise than in its establishment.

In a day when bloodshed is commonplace, the relative peace with which the reins of power in South Africa moved from the minority to the majority is a miracle. The leaders of the African National Congress (hereafter ANC) came to power with a desire for reconciliation and not revenge, as many had feared. Rather than embarking on a witch-hunt, they set up the Truth and Reconciliation Commission headed by Archbishop Desmond Tutu with a focus on forgiveness and justice. This too is a miracle, especially when one considers what all these people suffered and that their leader Nelson Mandela was, at best, vague about his religious convictions, even given a 630 page autobiography.[2] How could such a peaceful change have happened?

In their contribution to the construction and survival of the apartheid system, the Dutch Reformed Church (DRC) denied its own theological heritage. By supporting the government, its members were out to protect their own class interests, and so replaced their Reformed vision with a dualistic piety that sharply divided the world between the spiritual and the material. This enabled them in their thinking to serve God, in the church, even while they carried on their oppression in society.

We in the Christian Reformed Church (CRC) have also been guilty of suppressing our Reformed tradition for benefit of the general wealth and comfort of our members. We, too, have become dualistic and have domesticated and undermined our Reformed faith. We have turned away from our transforming vision for the whole world and have, instead, turned inward. This attitude is beginning to change, however, as evidenced, for example, by the work of the Office for Social Justice and Hunger Action, coordinated by

---

[1]I would like to acknowledge the helpful contribution of Wiebe K. Boer to this written response.
[2]*Long Walk to Freedom: The Autobiography of Nelson Mandela* (Johannesburg: Macdonald Purnell, 1994).

Peter Vander Meulen. This office is aimed at redirecting the CRC to its broader Reformed vision, as it calls for the liberation of the oppressed inside and outside our own society.

A comparison can also be made between American evangelicalism and South African evangelicalism. American evangelicals had learned to divide and conquer the black community in order to maintain their conservative power base. It is because of this that, in spite of the Christian leadership at the forefront of the Civil Rights Movement, that movement was still branded as non-Christian. Through expatriate missions, this brand of made-in-the-USA theology was exported to South Africa. South African evangelicals were similarly encouraged to be apolitical. Black evangelicals bought into this missionary piety and worried more about heaven and hell than about the inequality and injustice they faced on earth. They were forced to be politically irrelevant unless they broke away from their evangelical community.

Ironically, the ANC seemed to understand more about the power of Reformed theology and its ability to foster change than even the Dutch Reformed Church. They recognized the Christian call to engage culture, in contrast to the retreating pietism that was present in much of the African church and that was preventing it from playing a vital role in the national struggle. The ANC and their Communist allies recognized the church as a place that gives dignity to all and that has a basic commitment to justice. They, therefore, saw in the church a powerful institution that could bring the masses together as a forum in which to gain support for the liberation movement. Yet, they seemed to want to reap the benefits of this mass forum without accepting the true message of the church.

While the various Christian churches were divided among themselves, often ignoring the liberating power of the Gospel, the ANC recognized that power and attempted to use it for political advantage, yet without fully accepting its message. While South Africa's churches were calling for a heart change without a social and political change, this leading opposition group was calling for social and political change without recognizing the need for a change of heart.

From the intense dialogue going on in the World Council of Churches over Third World theologies of liberation, a relevant message for the world's oppressed peoples emerged. This ecumenical message was carried to South Africa by the likes of Archbishop Desmond Tutu. Other churches were also moved to see the need for a Christian faith and witness that involved more than just personal piety. Groups even emerged from the ranks of South African evangelicalism, as is evident by the publication of *Evangelical Witness in South Africa*, a fine document that denounces any stultifying dualism. The ecumenical world, the press, and the biblical witness conspired together to force evangelicals to reject their world-averting pietism and to work toward social transformation.

The rule of God in history became very evident as he brought all these disunified, misguided, and disparate groups together so that they could work as one toward a peaceful solution. God called out prophets and leaders from each group to dialogue. This led to the Rustenburg Conference in 1991, where the church publicly united to fight social injustice. It led to public confessions of the evils that had been perpetrated and to the recognition, most importantly, of the need for reconciliation. As Molebatsi tells us, the leaders of South Africa—both religious and political—knelt publicly before the cross, and in so doing acknowledged their dependence on God. After this, the church and the state could not go back. They committed themselves to the need for reconciliation, justice, restitution, peace, and transformation. The stage was set. The transition that only a few years before seemed impossible to attain within our lifetime took place over a short period of time and in relative peace.

The people of South Africa still have a long way to go in their quest for racial reconciliation. But this is true for all parts of the world, including our own United States and Canada. We, too, need to work for reconciliation and transformation within our society. The spirit of Rustenburg needs to be rekindled as we strive for reconciliation, justice, restitution, peace, and transformation—social realities we must not simply debate but that we must seek to realize. We must recognize where the divides exist in our society and use the weapons of Rustenburg for racial reconciliation. And we must do this in the realization that social change cannot take place without repentance.

Molebatsi's essay teaches us that the sovereignty of God is still present in political structures and historical events. It also teaches us that Christ's presence in culture, an important emphasis of Reformed theology, is a theme that needs to be underscored and realized within all societies, whether oppressed or free. Furthermore, we see that for theology to be relevant and applicable to a culture it must be understood by the masses. If these things are recognized, they will enable Christian leaders to unite and call any state to repentance, allowing in turn that nation to address the truly pressing issues that otherwise are lost in the midst of religious and political rhetoric and power struggles. South Africa is an example for us all of the power and social relevance of our Reformed tradition. Let us never allow ourselves to forget this.

Unity and Difference in Genesis 1

Richard J. Plantinga

IT IS NO easy matter to define *multiculturalism* or to specify exactly what it involves. In part, the difficulty involved in so doing is bound up with the root term *culture*, which is surely one of the least precise terms in the English language.[1] While defining and specifying multiculturalism is assuredly prerequisite to any progress that is to be made in this crucial area of Christian thinking and interacting, it is not my task to do so here. Rather, I would like to take this opportunity to say something about what I consider to be the chief theoretical issue that underlies multiculturalism and which the very title of this conference signals: the question of the One and the Many. No less a luminary than Hans-Georg Gadamer has indicated in his studies of Plato that this question in its many forms is one of the great philosophical questions of the ages.[2] The question of the One and the Many, moreover, is not just a philosophical issue: It is equally significant religiously and theologically. It is not accidental, therefore, that deliberation about it can be detected in many of the sacred texts of the world's great and philosophically sophisticated religious traditions, including the Hindu Upanishads, the Taoist Tao Te Ching, and the Christian Bible.

The heart of my brief remarks focuses on a sketch—and only a sketch— of some of the foundational resources for thinking about unity and plurality offered by the Bible and developed by the Christian tradition. While it is tempting to turn to certain passages in the New Testament in order to prompt theological reflection on diversity—Acts 2 readily suggests itself—I would instead like to concentrate my efforts on a crucial passage in the Old Testament. In so doing, I intend to draw attention to the preincarnational and pre-Pentecost wealth of biblical materials that are at the theologian's disposal for thinking about oneness and manyness.

The materials to which I draw attention are as far removed from the New Testament in terms of textual space as it is possible to be in the biblical narrative. Taking a theological cue from Karl Barth, who, according to his most able interpreter Eberhard Jüngel, insisted on always beginning again at the beginning,[3] I suggest that Genesis 1 provides basic orientation for reflection on the matter of unity and plurality insofar as it contains the nuclei

---

[1] A glance at a dictionary will indicate the semantic range of the term *culture*. See, for example, *Webster's New Collegiate Dictionary* (Springfield, Mass: G. & C. Merriam Company, 1979).
[2] See Gadamer's *Dialogue and Dialectic: Eight Hermeneutical Studies on Plato*, trans. P. C. Smith (New Haven: Yale University Press, 1980), 92, and *Reason In the Age of Science*, trans. F. G. Lawrence (Cambridge, Mass: MIT Press, 1983), 143.
[3] See Eberhard Jüngel, *Karl Barth: A Theological Legacy*, trans. G. E. Paul (Philadelphia: Westminster, 1986), 15, 27.

of three doctrines that are central to Christian belief and that are simultaneously indispensable for thinking about multiculturalism.

Consider the first four words of Genesis 1: "In the beginning God." Prior to creation, prior to the divine word that shattered the silence and emptiness of nonbeing, God is. In the unfolding of the biblical narrative and in subsequent reflection on it, the Christian Church came to confess its faith that the God who created in the beginning is none other than the triune God, who, according to the dictates of early Christian orthodoxy, is one in essence and three in person. If, therefore, the very being of God is somehow characterized by unity and plurality, the doctrine of God must surely provide some basic and suggestive clues for thinking about the One and the Many. While I cannot explore the rigors and intricacies of the doctrine of God as Trinity here, let alone its rich implications, I do wish to signal its centrality for thinking about multiculturalism, especially when seen in connection with other themes in Genesis 1.

Genesis 1 continues with the words "created the heavens and the earth." The triune God who alone *is* from eternity calls forth into being an ontologically distinct order, a realm of true otherness, made not out of the divine being or out of some other preexistent matter but out of nothing. This created reality, we learn as we continue to read in Genesis 1, is not only differentiated from God but differentiated intrinsically, that is "according to its kind." The light is therefore not the night, the sea is not the tree, and the dog is not the frog. What is striking about Genesis 1 is not just its reiteration of the theme of differentiation in creation, but its repeated pronouncement that creation in all its manifold variety and differentiation is good—prior, it should be noted, to the Fall recorded in Genesis 3.

The Genesis 1 text proceeds to relate the crowning achievement of the entire work of creation: the summoning forth of humanity crafted in the divine image. One would expect that at its most basic, the *imago Dei* would involve some kind of reflection, resemblance, or correspondence between Creator and creature—Barth's vehement protest notwithstanding. And so it is: Just as God is singular in essence and plural in person, so humanity shares one nature while existing as distinct persons, "male and female created he them" (v. 27). Thinking of the *imago Dei* as the *imago Trinitatis* fosters the recognition that each and every human being bears the divine image, a fact that indicates the basic equality of all persons. It also encourages the insight that there is a sense in which males and females socially comprise the image of God in a complementary, unifying, wholistically wonderful way—a way perceived and expressed in a somewhat unlikely source, namely, in *The Magic Flute* where Schikaneder/Mozart have Pamina and Papageno sing in one of the most sublime moments in all of art: "Man and woman and woman and man, To God attain—the noble plan."[4] The doctrine of the image of God

---

[4]Act one, no. 7, Duet ("Bei Männern, welche Liebe fühlen"). This rather free translation is my own, incorporating the intent of the previous two lines. The original

thus provides for human unity and equality, while simultaneously recognizing the propriety of created distinction and difference between persons.

The first human beings, having been thus ennobled with this lofty status, are then given a charge: "be fruitful, multiply, replenish, subdue, and have dominion" (v. 28). This *cultural* mandate represents the divine will for creation: Exercising divinely granted freedom and responsibility, human beings are to take care of creation, respect it, see that it flourishes, and tend and rule it wisely. In exploring the myriad of possibilities latent within the creation, humanity variously pours its being upon the given, graceful landscape. In other words, humanity is called to live an obedient and productive life of culture in the arena of nature, a dynamic eloquently described by Gerardus van der Leeuw in *Sacred and Profane Beauty* as follows:

> "Culture". . . [is] the domain of what is properly human, of the man who does not simply accept the world as he finds it, but rather transforms it into his own world. He makes of the steppes a farmland, of the forest a clearing in which he erects his house; he rides upon the waters; he makes of the music of the birds a song, of the movement of the animals a dance. Culture . . . is the movement of man through nature.[5]

Genesis 1 thus gives us the nuclei of three doctrines central to any orthodox, Christian confession and crucial for thinking about oneness and manyness, unity and plurality, and equality and diversity, namely these: (1) the doctrine of God as Trinity, in whom three equal persons are united in perichoretic love, will, and purpose; (2) the doctrine of creation, in which difference is not an evil to be overcome but a good to be embraced; and (3) the doctrine of humanity, in which human beings, who are themselves differentiated and who equally bear the image of the Trinity, are charged with the task of cultural formation in obedience to the divine will. What Genesis 1 teaches therefore is foundational: It is the great canvas on which the remainder of the biblical narrative is painted.

In time, we learn from the unfolding biblical story and especially from Genesis 3, unity *cum* differentiation would become disunity, and creational consonance would become dissonance: the divine and the human would become estranged from one another; humanity would become alienated from itself and from the rest of creation; and the task of cultural formation would

---

German reads:
>   Ihr [der Natur] hoher Zweck zeigt deutlich an:
>   Nicht Edlers sei, als Weib und Mann.
>   Mann und Weib, und Weib und Mann,
>   Reichen an die Gottheit an.

[5]Gerardus van der Leeuw, *Sacred and Profane Beauty: The Holy in Art*, trans. D. E. Green (New York: Holt, Rinehart and Winston, 1963), 13-14.

become misdirected and productive of disharmony. An ill-fated attempt to overcome this disunity is recorded in Genesis 11, as the peoples of the earth sought to construct a culturally disobedient, anthropocentrically based, and divinely hostile form of unity. This human attempt at unity was confounded by divinely sent linguistic plurality followed by confusion and dispersion.

The biblical text records that after Babel, God called Abram in order to make a great nation to be a light unto all the earth, setting off a chain of events that would lead to Bethlehem and Jerusalem, to incarnation and Pentecost, to divinely sent redemption in anticipation of re-creation. In other words, a new vision of unity is proffered later in the biblical text: The good news of divine-human reconciliation, of true unity, has been made available to all, male and female, Jew and Greek, Asian and American. This new and true unity is fostered by, ironically, divinely sent linguistic plurality followed not by confusion and dispersion, as in Genesis 11, but by the advent of one, holy, catholic church, as in Acts 2.

Theologically or prescriptively, therefore, what must be emphasized first and foremost regarding humanity, even as we know it in a broken world, is that the primary anthropological datum is the *imago Dei*, the fact that all human beings stand equally before the face of God. Secondary anthropological data, including particularities of race, ethnicity, gender, and ability are precisely that—secondary: significant but not first-order. Existentially or descriptively, however, what tends to be emphasized first and foremost regarding humanity as we know it in a broken world are secondary anthropological data. This *taxis* must be reversed. We must begin with unity and then go on to see and appreciate diversity, reminding ourselves that true otherness is a good and divine gift and that if God allowed for and delighted in such real over-againstness and difference in the beginning, it might well be paradigmatic for human beings to do likewise in the present.

Christianity therefore has powerful resources for addressing the question of the One and the Many and consequently for addressing multiculturalism. As to the Reformed tradition in particular, as part of the one, holy, catholic, and apostolic Church, it possesses many of the same resources as the rest of Christianity for addressing the challenge of plurality and is therefore well poised to contribute to ongoing multicultural conversation and practice in our time. But while all Christian communions confess belief in God the Father almighty who created heaven and earth, the Reformed tradition, when at its best, perhaps makes its particular contribution in accentuating the doctrine of creation in terms of its actual content, its relation to other doctrines, and its implications for life as well as thought. I have in this sense attempted a Reformed analysis in the sketch offered above. In addition to its confessional orthodoxy and vigorous theological tradition, finally, the Reformed tradition has an ongoing and principial willingness to change, as expressed in its dictum *ecclesia reformata semper reformanda est*. Consequently, its commitment to finding the One in the Many will surely continue, as continue it must, for the actual task is far from complete. In other words, if faith, to use

Simone Weil's beautiful words, is the experience that the intellect is enlightened by love, that love has yet to move the will to action.[6]

---

[6]In her *La Pesanteur et la Grâce* (Paris: Librairie Plon, 1948), Weil defines faith as follows: "La foi, c'est l'expérience que l'intelligence est éclairée par l'amour" (148). For a brief discussion of Weil's concept of faith, see George Grant, "Faith and the Multiversity" in *Technology and Justice* (Notre Dame: University of Notre Dame Press, 1986), 38ff.

Cultures and Communities of Higher Learning: Riding on the Bandwagon of Nonconformity

David A. Hoekema

THE TWO PERFORMERS were accompanied only by their own acoustic guitars, but their sound system was so bottom-heavy that I caught hardly any of the words they were singing. No matter. The fans who surrounded me in the Calvin Fieldhouse one evening in March 1997, knew the songs by heart. From time to time, while they played material from their early albums, the Indigo Girls stopped singing and let the crowd sing the lyrics for them.

So it was that I found myself in the midst of several thousand young women and men, all singing with one voice their songs of protest against social conformity, songs proclaiming the importance of each person's unique character and needs. The experience brought back to mind the concerts I had attended a quarter century ago, in the same fieldhouse, at which my contemporaries and I sang along with the protest songs of our own day, equally bent on being nonconformists just like all the people we admired.

The world of higher education today has something in common with this ironic ceremony of shared nonconformity. Diversity and multiculturalism are the bywords of the day. When I accompanied my son recently on a quick tour of college World Wide Web sites, it was evident that multiculturalism, once the rallying cry of those who felt excluded from the halls of academe, has become an essential ingredient in the public identity of nearly every institution. A college that does not proclaim the diversity of its student body is as rare as a tube of toothpaste without fluoride. Multiculturalism has become the oat bran of contemporary higher education.

Looking for grist for my mill in preparing this essay, I conducted a search for material on "diversity, multiculturalism, and higher education" using one of the leading Internet search engines. It produced thirty-six documents for the year 1994. For 1995 there were two hundred, and for 1996 the number soared to well over one thousand. One of them was a review of *Gale's Encyclopedia of Multiculturalism*, a two-volume work published in 1995. The reviewer, a reference librarian, observed that the new work is a useful complement to two other encyclopedias in the same general area that have appeared in the past four years. Spawning three encyclopedias is a vivid indication of the breadth of interest in multicultural topics and of how rapidly multiculturalism has gained its prominent place in contemporary academic discourse.

When we dedicate ourselves to a deeper exploration of multiculturalism, as Calvin College has done throughout the 1996-1997 school year, we need to ask whether we are merely jumping on the bandwagon of nonconformity, as I have put it in my title. The complaint of feminists, social historians, Asianists, and Africanists that the traditional canon excludes the history and experience of most of the people of the world has by now been heard on nearly every campus. Alice Walker's *The Color Purple* was the single most frequently assigned text in American college classrooms a few years ago. Iconoclasm is trendy, and institutions of higher education seem to exhibit nearly as strong a herd instinct as any crowd of adolescent concertgoers. Every institution now wants to be unlike all those other colleges, mired in tradition, that study only the work of dead white males. The places on the periphery of the curriculum from which these critiques were launched are becoming crowded. Some observers go so far as to claim that dissent from the dominant Western canon has become the new orthodoxy. The cultural blinders that supposedly once kept students from noticing anything that lay outside the mainstream of the dominant Western intellectual tradition have merely been replaced by another set of blinders with equivalent but opposite biases, say these critics.

A leading voice in this chorus has been that of think-tank scholar Dinesh D'Souza, who brought his campaign against the ideology of multiculturalism to Calvin in 1991 as a January Series speaker. Writing in *Forbes* magazine a few months later, D'Souza claimed that "liberal arts students, including those attending Ivy League schools, are very likely to be exposed to an attempted brainwashing that deprecates Western learning and exalts a neo-Marxist ideology promoted in the name of multiculturalism."[1] Furthermore, he charged, universities' "appeasement gestures" to satisfy "the political demands of victim groups," such as preferential admission and separate housing options for minority students, "create a kind of academic apartheid." He supported these charges in his book *Illiberal Education* with a succession of horror stories from eminent universities and colleges—Harvard, Duke, Texas, SUNY—in which conservative faculty and students had been silenced and ostracized.[2]

The book became one of the best-selling books on higher education of the decade, and its message was heard in the halls of government no less than of academia. In May 1991, for example, President George Bush chose to use the occasion of his commencement address at the University of Michigan to warn against the threat of leftist intolerance. "On the 200th anniversary of our Bill of Rights," he said, "we find free speech under assault throughout the United States, including on some college campuses," referring to attempts to bar speech that defames women, minorities, and homosexuals. "In their own

---

[1] Dinesh D'Souza, "The Visigoths in Tweed," *Forbes*, 1 April 1991; reprinted in Patricia Aufderheide, ed., *Beyond P.C.: Toward a Politics of Understanding* (St. Paul, Minn.: Greywolf Press, 1992), 12.
[2] Dinesh D'Souza, *Illiberal Education: The Politics of Race and Sex on Campus* (New York: Macmillan, 1991).

Orwellian way," he warned, "crusades that demand correct behavior crush diversity in the name of diversity."[3]

Unfortunately D'Souza's zeal to uphold tradition outran his faithfulness to the facts. The eminent historian C. Vann Woodward, even while sharing D'Souza's conservative stance and decrying the ideological excesses of multiculturalism, wrote of his disappointment with D'Souza's book in July 1991, in *The New York Review of Books*. At first, he wrote, "I accepted its purely factual statements as true," but on closer examination "the book turned out to contain some serious and irresponsible factual errors."[4] Woodward argues, all the same, that D'Souza has done the academy a service by opening up for honest discussion a topic previously treated only with evasion and dishonesty on the part of university administrators. Others who ferreted out the facts behind his case studies were less charitable. Jon Wiener concluded after interviewing all the principals in a Harvard incident supposedly involving trumped-up charges of racism, "If D'Souza's account of the Thernstrom case is typical of his work, *Illiberal Education* rests on a morass of inaccuracies, exaggerations, and falsehoods."[5]

It is not my purpose here to attempt to settle the still-simmering dispute over whether "political correctness" on campus is rampant or rare—whether it is an intellectual Ebola virus attacking the very flesh of the academy or a phantasm created by reactionary demagogues. Without a doubt, multiculturalist principles have sometimes been invoked in defense of shoddiness and ideological distortion. Recall the Afrocentric curriculum introduced a few years ago into California schools, which made implausible and groundless claims to the effect that nearly every advance in ancient Western religion, art, and science was borrowed from superior African civilizations. D'Souza holds up for ridicule a past president of the Stanford Black Student Union who complained that "I read the Bible without knowing St. Augustine looked black like me, that the 10 Commandments were almost direct copies" from an Egyptian code.[6] In fact, Augustine was probably an olive-skinned Berber, and there is no more about him in the Bible than there is about Benjamin Franklin; and the links between the Decalogue and any Egyptian code are tenuous and debatable. If nonsense such as this is the best that higher learning can produce, should we spend tuition or tax dollars to support it?

---

[3]George Bush, "Remarks at the University of Michigan Commencement Ceremony in Ann Arbor, May 4, 1991"; reprinted in Aufderheide, *Beyond P.C.*, 227.
[4]C. Vann Woodward, "Freedom and the Universities," *New York Review of Books*, 18 July 1991; reprinted, with corrections and updated information provided by the author, in Aufderheide, *Beyond P.C.*, 29.
[5]Jon Wiener, "What Happened at Harvard," *The Nation*, 30 September 1991; reprinted in Aufderheide, *Beyond P.C.*, 105.
[6]D'Souza, *Illiberal Education*, 66.

But the charge that such ignorance and irresponsibility run rampant on university campuses does not hold up on closer examination. The Afrocentric curriculum that D'Souza rightly criticizes, for example, has been used by very few schools, and it has come under scathing criticism from the advocates of multiculturalism no less than from its critics. Ignorance and overconfidence are in rich supply on every campus (except Calvin's), and they are not limited to students of a particular ethnic group or political stripe. Multiculturalists hold no monopoly on wrong-headed or error-riddled curricular materials, nor have its advocates been exempt from their colleagues' critical questions. The claim that multiculturalism fosters mediocrity and sloganeering turns out to rest on selective and exaggerated argument by anecdote.

Yet, even though D'Souza's accusations of pervasive liberal bias in academia are highly dubious, he has identified accurately the two distinct but interrelated issues that make multiculturalism such a contentious issue on campuses today. They can be summarized as follows: First, has multiculturalism brought about a revolution in the liberal-arts curriculum, and, if so, is it a revolution for the better or for the worse? Second, has the emphasis on multicultural sensitivity and student diversity brought a revolution in campus life, and, if so, has the change been a boon or a bane? In the remainder of my comments today I will attempt, in a variety of direct and indirect ways, to provide answers to these two questions.

I begin with the second: How has multiculturalism changed student life? Profound changes in the demographics of higher education have brought a very different group of students to our campuses in the 1990s than were present a generation earlier. In 1960, for example, 94 percent of college students were white, and of the remaining 6 percent, a third attended predominantly black institutions. Men accounted for 63 percent of the student population. In 1991, men represented only 45 percent, and white students 80 percent, of college students. Changes at Calvin have been less dramatic, but they show the same overall pattern. North American minority students made up less than 2 percent of Calvin's student body through the 1970s and halfway through the 1980s, followed by a gradual increase to about 4 percent in the 1990s. Men were barely a majority in 1975, where today they are a minority of 44 percent. International enrollment has grown from 1.6 percent in 1975 to 3 percent in 1990, then declined somewhat to 2.3 percent in 1996.

Inevitably the change in who attends college—larger numbers of women, American ethnic minorities, foreign students, and larger numbers in aggregate—have brought about changes and created tensions in student social patterns. A subtle but pervasive racial tension has been described vividly by Berkeley sociologist Troy Duster in summarizing the outcome of an extensive study of race relations among students on his campus:

> What our hundreds of interviews showed is that there is a sharp difference between the ways black and white students feel about racial politics; Asians and Chicanos fall somewhere in between.

> White students tend to arrive with an almost naive goodwill, as if they are saying, "I think I'll just go and have some diversity," while music from *Peter and the Wolf* plays in the background. They expect to experience the "other" without conflict, without tension, without anything resembling bitterness or hostility. Meanwhile, many blacks arrive after being told in high school that Berkeley is a tough place, an alien environment, and that in order to survive, they should stick with other black people.
>
> Imagine then what happens in the first few weeks of the first semester. White students looking for diversity run into black students already sure that race is political, so pick your friends carefully. White students seeking easy access to a black group can quickly find their hands slapped. They might say something offensive without knowing it and get called "racist," a word they use to mean prejudging a person because he or she is black. *Why do you call me racist? Hey, I'm willing to talk to you like an ordinary person.*
>
> But when black students use the term, they tend to aim it at a person they see participating in a larger institution that works against black people. *If you're not in favor of affirmative action, that means you're racist.*
>
> The white student retorts: *I'm willing to have dinner with you, talk with you about ideas. I'm not prejudiced.* But the two are talking past each other, the white student describing a style of interaction and friendship, the black student about the set of views the white student appears to hold.[7]

The result has been a phenomenon that conservative critics have observed but misattributed to a "politics of appeasement," namely, a pattern of social segregation that has persisted despite institutional efforts for integration. At the University of Delaware, where I was a professor of philosophy until 1992, I seldom saw racially mixed groups of students in the student union during lunch hour or after classes. In the classroom and in student government, students of all races worked side by side; but in social settings they tended to separate, like different liquids that can be shaken together but are not mutually soluble.

This pattern seems less evident at Calvin. In the student commons, in my experience, it is rare to see a table occupied only by minority students, but it is quite common to see one or two African American or Asian American students sitting down with a group of white classmates. Groups of friends still seem to separate to some extent along ethnic lines, but the barriers appear more permeable here than on many campuses. I hope that this reflects an

---

[7]Troy Duster, "Beyond the Myths," in Aufderheide, *Beyond P.C.*, 183-84.

openness and mutual respect that will persist as we continue our efforts to build an ethnically diverse student body.

I have not yet addressed the question of whether changes in student culture are for the better or for the worse, nor have I touched on the question of whether multiculturalism has brought major changes to the curriculum. Let me answer those questions indirectly by posing some other questions. First I want to pose three questions that have easy answers. Then I will follow them with two questions that are much harder to answer. To the first three, I will provide answers. The others I may have to leave as a homework assignment.

First, *should we work to achieve a more diverse and more ethnically integrated atmosphere on campus*? The answer is easy: Yes, we should. To see why, we need only look at the sorry record of racial segregation in the United States—segregation long removed from the law and yet stubbornly preserved by economic and social forces. For reasons of pragmatic politics as well as moral principle, we ought to strive to make our campuses models of how students from a broad range of cultural, social, and economic circumstances can live, learn, and work together effectively.

Troy Duster responds as follows to the critics of the university critics who point to racial tensions on his campus as a sign of failure, a sign that diversity is not working:

> But there is another, more hopeful interpretation. Berkeley's students are grappling with one of the most difficult situations in the world: ethnic and racial turf. They are doing this, however modestly, over relatively safe issues such as what kind of music gets played or who sits where in the lunchroom. Perhaps they will learn how to handle conflict, how to divvy up scarce resources, how to adjust, fight, retreat, compromise, and ultimately get along in a future that will no longer be dominated by a single group spouting its own values as the ideal homogenized reality for everyone else. If our students learn even a small bit of this, they will be far better prepared than students tucked safely away in anachronistic single-culture enclaves. And what they learn may make a difference not just for their personal future, but for a world struggling with issues of nationalism, race, and ethnicity.[8]

Rather than dwell on persistent failures to create an inclusive and integrated community, we should instead be thankful that our campuses, including this one, are substantially more representative of the numerous racial, ethnic, and economic groups in our society than they were a generation ago. And we should rededicate ourselves to making this fragile experiment in living together succeed.

It is particularly important to rededicate ourselves to this goal in light of the sustained attack on affirmative-action programs of every sort that is being

---

[8]Ibid., 184.

waged all around us in legislatures, courts, and editorial pages. A ballot initiative in California that prohibits all consideration of race and gender in admissions decisions by public universities drew a substantial majority, only to be blocked by a court order—and then reinstated in April 1997, when an appeals court issued a blistering rebuke to the lower court about interfering with democratic processes. Even longtime advocates of race-based affirmative action such as Derrick Bell of Harvard Law School now call for nonracial policies of assistance based on economic and social disadvantage and on evidence of motivation to succeed, rather than politically doomed policies sensitive to race, as the only remaining route to diversity. We may well achieve our purposes better by broadening our view of social advantage in this way—even if we dissent from Bell's cynical view that the gates are slamming shut on minorities precisely in order to ensure that diversity remains a public-relations ploy to protect entrenched economic and political power from serious challenge.[9] The members of the American Association of Universities, sixty-two of the leading public and private universities, passed a resolution on April 14, 1997, and took out a display advertisement in *The New York Times* on April 24 to reaffirm in the face of recent attacks the "continuing need to take into account a wide range of considerations—including ethnicity, race, and gender—as we evaluate students whom we select for admission."[10]

In this highly charged political climate, it is all the more important for us at Calvin College to say forthrightly and unambiguously: We will pursue the goal of racial and ethnic diversity because we believe it helps us all to learn from each other and to understand the global dimensions of Christ's kingdom. We will not pursue that goal in ways that are discriminatory or unfair, but neither will we allow an abstract ideal of color blindness to impede our efforts to build such a community of learning. Our common goals are more important than meeting the political tests of either the left or the right.

Here is my second essay question, *should the canon around which liberal education is built be open to change in response to multicultural challenges?* The answer, again, is yes. The answer has always been yes, for as long as there has been a canon. There is nothing unique about the challenges brought by feminists, Marxists, Africanists, and others, for what we now regard as the established corpus of the Western tradition is itself the result of hotly contested arguments in previous generations.

What is the history of Western music without Bach, we may ask? Without Mendelssohn's advocacy in the nineteenth century, Bach might have remained forever lost in obscurity, no more a household name than Joachim

---

[9]Derrick Bell, "Protecting Diversity Programs from Political and Judicial Attack," *Chronicle of Higher Education*, 4 April 1997, B4-5.
[10]"On the Importance of Diversity in University Admissions," paid advertisement, *The New York Times*, 24 April 1997, A17.

Quantz or Karl Ditters von Dittersdorf. How dare today's iconoclasts place Toni Morrison or Derek Walcott on the pedestal of great literature, alongside Melville and Whitman? Not long ago Melville and Whitman were suspect, but Alfred Lord Tennyson and John Greenleaf Whittier were the exemplars of greatness. Even today, change comes slowly. In the midst of all the furor over the radicalization of the curriculum, a survey of nearly a thousand English departments conducted by the Modern Language Association found that key upper-level literature courses had undergone only small changes in the list of authors assigned and in the attention given to historical and cultural background. Fewer than one-quarter of faculty respondents at four-year colleges said that Marxist approaches influenced their teaching, and only 16 percent cited poststructuralism as an influence. Dickens and Eliot still dominate assignments in British literature, Emerson and Hawthorne and Melville the American reading list, and there is "no evidence that English faculty members have abandoned traditional texts."[11]

The canon is perpetually under challenge and open to revision, and it is foolish to pretend that we can freeze it forever within its present boundaries. Only a person possessing the supreme self-assurance of a Mortimer Adler dares to pronounce that although some writings by minority authors deserve a place among the "good books" of Western civilization, none attains the status of "great books" that "are relevant to human problems in every century."[12] For those of us who claim no such Olympian wisdom, it is presumptuous and futile to decry changes in the canon. Innovation itself reinforces tradition in many ways. Derek Walcott's Caribbean epic poetry sends us back to Homer with eyes open a little wider, and the plays of Athol Fugard and Lanford Wilson invite us to look again at ancient Greek drama and at Aristotle's theory of catharsis through imitation.

My next "easy question" isn't quite so easy, and answering it will lead us into the hard questions. Third, *are ethnic diversity and multiculturalism valuable in themselves?* In the academy today these are often taken as inherent goods, desirable for their own sake. This is a mistake. They are not inherent but instrumental goods, goals that are important because they help institutions achieve more fundamental purposes. A community characterized by racial, ethnic, and economic diversity is valuable because such a community brings us nearer to our larger goals.

The goal toward which all of our programs and policies at Calvin are directed is, in shortest compass, the preparation of young men and women for lives of Christian service. Our purpose as an institution is to help students become active, critical, and effective participants in the concentric circles of

---

[11] Phyllis Franklin, Bettina Huber, and David Laurence, "Continuity and Change in the Study of Literature," *Change*, January/February 1992, 43-48.
[12] Mortimer Adler, "The Transcultural and the Multicultural," in *The Great Ideas Today* (Chicago: Encyclopedia Britannica, 1991); quoted in Auferdeide, *Beyond P.C.*, 60.

family, church, and society, building on a firm foundation of knowledge and moved by a love for others and a passion for justice.

We can work toward this goal no matter how exclusive or inclusive our community may be. But homogeneity and insularity discourage any independent and critical engagement with the society around us, and they foster the illusion that the world is predictable and familiar. In Lake Wobegon, the Sidetrack Tap is described as "the place to go that's just like home, if you were brought up that way." Some Christian colleges seem to strive to be a place just like home, set apart from the secular world, and they therefore place little importance on diversity.

Should we embrace this model? It would save a lot of frustrating efforts to recruit students and faculty more broadly. It is not inherently wrong, or contrary to Christian principles, but it is deeply at odds with Calvin's goal of preparing students to be a transformative presence in a pluralistic and increasingly fragmented society. That goal can best be pursued by making our own campus a model of a diverse, compassionate, and committed Christian community. Multiculturalism is a needed means to the end of providing a challenging and rigorous preparation for subsequent service, not an independent goal in itself. But this leads us to another question, one that admits no easy or unqualified answer:

Fourth, *should our curriculum become distinctively multicultural?* This is a contentious question, one over which faculty on many campuses have lined up in opposing camps. During the 1997-98 year, a committee of wise and experienced colleagues will be devoting a great deal of reflection to this question, among others, in the context of Calvin's core curriculum. I will not presume to draw their conclusions for them but instead will offer only a brief retrospective observation.

The curriculum at Calvin has already become markedly multicultural in several respects. Growing numbers of students now integrate foreign study into their core and major studies. Rapid growth in academically based service offerings, motivated more by a desire to integrate learning and doing, have also effectively extended our classrooms into a wide range of local communities, as students go out into schools, community-service agencies, and retirement homes to complete their service requirements. There has also been a significant enrichment of history, English, philosophy, and nursing courses with texts and topics drawn from non-Western sources and from previously excluded groups in Western society.

Colleagues and students would agree, I think, that these are areas of strength, not weakness, in our current curriculum. Conservative critics would find little grist for their mill in Calvin's courses, which have opened doors to diverse communities without compromising academic demands. There is room for much more to be done, however. My department, philosophy, offers few courses that highlight the philosophical contributions of non-Western cultures. Calvin's division of natural science and mathematics offers only a handful of courses, mostly electives rather than requirements, in which students gain a historical and cultural perspective on non-Western science and technology. I hope that the core study committee, and departments across campus as well, will focus on a variety of ways in which a multicultural emphasis can strengthen and not weaken or dilute our curriculum.

Fifth, *should our diversity be like everybody else's diversity?* In other words, returning to the concert scene with which I opened, should we strive to be nonconformists just like everyone else? Clearly we should not. We must guard against the temptation to jump on the bandwagon of nonconformity and fashion our efforts for diversity on the models that are most familiar in the higher-education marketplace. Calvin is in a unique position to assert, and to exemplify, something too often ignored in the contemporary debate over cultural pluralism: Diversity among institutions of higher education is no less important than diversity within each of them. As we strive to expand the horizons of our students and to draw students to Calvin from a wider range of religious and educational backgrounds, we must remember that Calvin is committed to a unique Reformed vision of intellectual and spiritual integrity that calls us to direct the light of the Gospel into every corner of contemporary society. What fits other excellent liberal-arts colleges may not fit Calvin's distinctive mission. Policies and goals embraced by peers among Christian colleges may also fall short of Calvin's ideals.

What does this mean in practical terms? We need to be honest, in the first place, about the uniqueness of a college with ethnic as well as theological roots. Even as the percentage of students and faculty drawn from communities of Dutch immigrants continues to decline, vestiges of that tradition remain visible in our customs and folkways. Even campus slang gives us away—when professors mutter that they are *benauwd* (stifled, oppressed) or refer to a visit from the dean as *huisbezoek* (parish visitation). Some commuting students still label themselves "GR biters," a Dutch-English descendent of *buitenlanders* (foreigners), those who commute from outside the city. We cannot put this ethnic heritage completely behind us, nor should we attempt to do so, even while we offer as warm a welcome as possible to colleagues and students who know nothing of this odd little enclave in American Protestantism. We need to distinguish carefully between those elements of the college's Dutch American heritage that contribute to a distinctive culture of inquiry, on the one hand, and those that merely alienate newcomers, on the other.

The historic ties that limit our diversity in some ways also open doors closed to others. The Calvin campus is enriched by the presence of faculty colleagues and visitors from Nigeria, South Africa, the Netherlands, Hungary, and other countries in which the Reformed churches have an active presence. The far-flung mission fields of our sponsoring denomination bring students to us from around the globe.

I have noticed a surprising pattern in students who have come to Calvin from the mission fields where Reformed churches are active. Those who are themselves African or Asian, having learned how to work with American church representatives in the mission setting and having consciously decided to pursue their studies in a foreign culture, seem to feel more readily at home at Calvin than do African American or Asian American students who have traveled a much shorter distance. Children of American mission and relief workers, for their part, seem to be keenly attuned to issues of global justice and American complacency. They are often more critical of Calvin's customs and of American ways, and less comfortable in their new milieu, than are their classmates who have spent their entire lives on American soil.

Out of the rich ethnic and religious mixture that characterizes mission work today comes a unique opportunity to draw diverse cultures into fruitful dialogue and interchange on Calvin's campus. A vivid example of such sharing can be found in the chapels led by foreign students and in the now annual Rangeela celebration of the performing arts. By attracting larger numbers from church mission fields, and by highlighting their contributions to our community, Calvin can achieve an unusual kind of diversity and a level of intercultural dialogue that no secular college can ever duplicate.

Calvin has unique obstacles to overcome, and unique advantages on which it can draw in achieving kinds of diversity that fit its mission and situation. If we dedicate ourselves anew, at the close of our first multicultural year, to the articulation and achievement of distinctive modes of diversity in students, faculty, and programs, goals that go beyond the mere addition of nonwhite faces to the classroom, we will be in a position to provide leadership in American higher education. We can carry high the standard of distinctively Christian higher education that translates into a daily campus reality the vision of God's kingdom as encompassing every people and nation. That is a far more difficult, but also a far more worthwhile, endeavor than merely jumping aboard the diversity bandwagon.

It is a costly endeavor in many ways. Faculty and staff and students as well must work constantly to attract a diverse student body and faculty and to build a supportive environment on our campus. We need to listen to dissenting voices, like that of the student who complained in our student newspaper *Chimes* recently about the unfairness of multicultural scholarships for adopted children. We must not assume that our policies are right simply because they aim at worthy goals—or that the policies that have helped us advance to our present situation will serve us well for the future. Yet the costs and the difficulties are far outweighed by the benefits that accrue to all of us in a community in which many nations and colors and modes of cultural and intellectual life come together.

Like the students at the Indigo Girls concert, colleges take comfort in singing familiar words to the same tune. The challenge that lies before Calvin today, as we seek to translate a year of cultural enrichment into a renewed and transformed learning environment, is to find new ways of opening our classrooms outward into a world in which people of every race and nation work side by side in an atmosphere of openness and mutual respect.

Civil rights leader Roger Wilkins has described his experience as one of a handful of black students at the University of Michigan in the early 1950s, where they "were made to feel like partly welcome guests, grudgingly accepted." Despite the success of a few black students in rising to positions of leadership, writes Wilkins:

> Michigan taught one overwhelming racial lesson: blacks were peripheral to the life of the nation, and their capacities to contribute were limited at best. That was a heavy burden for our young black souls to bear, and I'm sure it did some of us permanent damage.
>
> But the white kids were at least as severely damaged. They were learning the same lessons about the capacities and human worth of people of color. Michigan wasn't unique. That was the traditional way for whites to be trained nationwide. Some people wondered why, in the next decade, the country's "best and brightest" couldn't accurately assess the political and fighting abilities of the Vietnamese enemy. I was never puzzled because I had seen how they had been educated.[13]

White students of the 1950s were damaged no less than black students, Wilkins observes. Similarly, today we owe it to students from the majority culture no less than to those drawn from minority groups to offer an education that highlights the contributions of many peoples and cultures to our world and to the disciplines and theories through which we come to understand it. We need to learn not to sing the same song together but rather to sing different songs and to hear different harmonies as they emerge from the intertwining and crisscrossing melodies. If we tune first our ears, and then our voices, to the many kinds of music found in the many cultures of our own land—Anglo, Hispanic, African American, Asian American; if we strain our ears to hear what it is like to experience the world as a Nigerian or Korean or Iranian; if we commit ourselves as a community to encouraging a rich chorus of different songs—if we do all this, then we will not only graduate students who are able to understand and resolve the challenges of a multicultural world; even more importantly, we will be declaring, for all the world to see, that we belong to "a great multitude . . . from every nation, from all tribes and peoples and languages, standing before the throne and before the Lamb."[14]

---

[13] Roger Wilkins, A Modern Story," *Mother Jones*, September/October 1991; reprinted in Aufderheide, *Beyond P.C.*, 163.
[14] Rev. 7:9, New Revised Standard Version.

Multicultural Openness and Victimization: A Response to David A. Hoekema

Cornelius Plantinga Jr.

DAVID HOEKEMA'S ESSAY is both lively and thoughtful. As an additional advantage, it is right. I am therefore able to spare readers by making only brief and ancillary comments. I'll make three of these and then add a remark on a matter raised by Thomas Thompson and Leanne Van Dyk.

First, in his book entitled *Dictatorship of Virtue: Multiculturalism and the Battle for America's Future*,[1] Richard Bernstein tells of a lecture in Brooklyn, Massachusetts in October of 1990 by an educational consultant named Peggy Means McIntosh. McIntosh was lecturing a group of elementary teachers on the need to avoid "pinnacling" in education, a scheme in which people try to mount up the pinnacles of learning by getting answers (as in arithmetic) "right" instead of "wrong." When trapped by this scheme children might, for example, multiply 42 by 43 and privilege 1806 by calling it "right."

But this "either/or, right/wrong, you got it/you don't" approach to education is a faulty paradigm, said McIntosh, for it obliges children to accept the cultural hegemony of objective rightness. Better, she offered, to "put the child in a lateral relation to her own learning, beyond win-lose.... Then we could see learning not as mastery but as our connection with the world, as we grow and develop as bodies in the body of the world."[2]

Hoekema cautions against simply believing all such stories of multicultural wackiness on the nation's campuses and in its school systems. I think he is right to do so. Some of these stories may be true, but some may also be false (or perhaps "false"), and we will therefore do well to put many of them into suspension. Perhaps the pinnacling story, for example, belongs in suspension.

And maybe, while we're at it, we ought to suspend a second story. According to Peter Collier and David Horowitz in *Destructive Generation: Second Thoughts about the Sixties*[3] the Berkeley, California schoolboard once introduced the story of Little Red Riding Hood into the schools' peace curriculum as "an exercise in failed conflict resolution." The Board's idea was that the wolf and Ms. Hood failed to explore ways in which they could have "settled their differences amicably," perhaps by a compromise according to which the wolf would surrender his tendencies toward carnivorousness while Ms. Hood would surrender her stereotypes of wolves.[4]

Following Hoekema's lead, I suggest that we neither believe nor disbelieve such stories, but instead simply savor them as piquant and

---

[1] New York: Knopf, 1994.
[2] Ibid., 252-53.
[3] New York: Summit Books, 1990.
[4] Ibid., 239.

toothsome. Nonetheless, as these stories remind us, the debate over multiculturalism in contemporary America has to do not just with inclusiveness, let alone with inclusiveness where the canon of literature is concerned. It has to do as well with basic ways of knowing and judging truth, including moral truth. Indeed, the debate centers for such critics as Bernstein on whether multiculturalism has, here or there, moved beyond a so-called "sensibility of openness" to become a political program of so hard a texture that only laughter can soften it.

Second, on the canon and what ought to be there, Hoekema thinks this is worth arguing about, but it isn't worth worrying about. After all, the vicissitudes of selecting a canon are old and familiar. Authors normally come into and go out of fashion and, in any case, innovation often reinforces tradition. Fair enough. But we ought also to ask ourselves what we should want from a revised canon. What are we trying to accomplish with it?

I hope we would be trying to help students learn to love. One would think that this would be the main idea in a multicultural reading program, but, as Katha Pollitt once observed, these programs sometimes have a medicinal feel to them, as if the problem with students is that they are all afflicted with the wrong biases and need a good dose of this or that reading prescription to suppress their biases and to adopt those of the person who wrote the prescription. Depending on who the person is, this might not be such a bad idea, but in any case it's important to keep a light hand here. Reading is for joy and for instruction. It is also for learning to love. As Caroline Simon says in *The Disciplined Heart*,[5] thoughtful reading is a matrix of love. Love doesn't always emerge from this matrix (some tyrants have been heavy readers), but Christians intend it to emerge. A Christian reads fiction as a spiritual discipline.

So at Calvin College we should amiably negotiate and renegotiate the canon. (Students will anyhow read other things besides the ones we assign.) What we must not negotiate is the attitude of alert interest and openness to the lives of others that we want to awaken by reading.

Third, Hoekema rightly states that diversity among institutions of higher learning is just as important as diversity within them. This is an important observation. The point of it, sharpened here by Hoekema, was made at the beginning of Calvin's multicultural year by Justo González in his speech to the college faculty. The point is that to reach out you need a base. You have to know who you are. To offer hospitality you need a home, and the home ought not to look like a motel room. It ought to look and feel like your living place, the place that you indwell. Thus, if the University of Notre Dame has an Irish Catholic feel to it, and if St. Olaf College has a Norwegian Lutheran feel to it, and if Calvin College has a Dutch Reformed feel to it, so be it—just so long as each institution also makes space for others and helps them to flourish in that space.

---

[5] Grand Rapids: Eerdmans, 1997

Finally, in an essay of rare power and beauty, Thompson proposes that in imitation of Christ we ought to surrender ourselves, give up ourselves, empty ourselves of pride and self-justification. In an instructive comment Van Dyk observes that certain people—the impoverished, the tyrannized, the diminished—have had their emptying done for them by others, so that they no longer possess much by way of pride to give up.

True enough. In cases—such as in the cases of some women—where people have been humiliated, it is both cruel and irrelevant to preach humility to them, and Van Dyk is right to point this out.

But it's not cruel or irrelevant to preach justification by grace alone. Here, it seems to me, Thompson's thesis applies more widely than we might initially suppose, for in the alchemy of sin even lowliness can become our justifying distinction. In Dickens' *David Copperfield*, for example, Uriah Heep turns his 'umble status and his capacity for "eating 'umble pie with an appetite" into leverage on his superiors. He knows they want 'umbleness in their inferiors and Uriah Heep gives them all they want. Here is a will-to-power as strong and as manipulative as anything you could find in a patrician slumlord. The same dynamic may be seen among members of oppressed groups who adopt an in-your-face form of exhibitionism that is meant to offend, and among groups who get locked into "lowlier than thou" contests in which the prize is recognition, sometimes approaching celebration, of one's victimhood. "I'm somebody to reckon with" is said by dominant persons and groups, but also, sometimes, by their victims. The dominant have no monopoly on self-justification. And no person or group can sidestep the need for salvation by grace alone.

The Comprehensive Plan: What Have We Accomplished?

Steven R. Timmermans

THE PURPOSE OF this symposium is to provide a concluding synthesis of Calvin's Multicultural Year. The proposal for a Multicultural Year came from the Multicultural Affairs Committee and was adopted by the Faculty Senate in January of 1996, almost exactly ten years after the Comprehensive Plan was adopted by the faculty on January 27, 1986. In making its proposal, the Multicultural Affairs Committee stated that "it is necessary in this ten-year anniversary time to bring renewed attention to these goals [of the Comprehensive Plan] and to strive for recommitment [to them]."[1] Thus, in this second day of the symposium, it is appropriate to focus our attention on *The Comprehensive Plan for Integrating North American Ethnic Minority Persons and Their Interests into Every Facet of Calvin's Institutional Life*.[2] My title, "The Comprehensive Plan: What Have We Accomplished?" asks an evaluative question. It is my intent to answer that question and to offer a tentative explanation both for our accomplishments and the lack thereof.

The Comprehensive Plan identifies four critical areas for integrating ethnic minorities into Calvin's institutional life: (1) faculty and staff: recruitment, retention and community life; (2) students: recruitment, retention and student life; (3) the broader Christian community; and (4) curriculum. For each of these areas the authors of the Comprehensive Plan included goals and strategies for change. My treatment of each area will be selective and in no respect exhaustive.[3]

In considering the Comprehensive Plan it is important also to consult related college policy statements and position papers, such as the statement adopted by the faculty in 1993 describing Calvin College as a multicultural academic community,[4] the revised description of the position of Director of Academic Multicultural Affairs, which deviates significantly from the description provided in the Comprehensive Plan,[5] and Appendix Y of the

---

[1] Multicultural Affairs Committee, *Designation of Academic Year 1996-97 as a Multicultural Year* (Grand Rapids: Calvin College, 1996), 1.
[2] Minority Concerns Task Force, *The Comprehensive Plan for Integrating North American Ethnic Minority Persons and Their Interests into Every Facet of Calvin's Institutional Life* (Grand Rapids: Calvin College, 1985); hereafter, Comprehensive Plan.
[3] For a brief overview of the Comprehensive Plan, see the Appendix to this volume, which reproduces the introductory summary section of the Comprehensive Plan.
[4] *Calvin College as a Multicultural Academic Community* (Grand Rapids: Calvin College, 1993).
[5] Multicultural Affairs Committee, *Academic Multicultural Affairs Administrators* (Grand Rapids: Calvin College, 1990).

Handbook for Teaching Faculty, which includes background and policy adopted prior to the Comprehensive Plan.[6]

In answering the question that my title asks, I must first thank a number of people who contributed to this report. During the previous academic year, the Multicultural Affairs Committee reviewed and evaluated the many recommendations found within the Comprehensive Plan by soliciting the assessment of individuals responsible for their implementation. Those reporting to the committee included Provost Gordon Van Harn, Vice President Jeanette DeJong, Vice President Thomas McWhertor, Dean Frank Roberts, Dean David Hoekema, and Human Resources Director Constance Bellows.

The Broader Christian Community

I begin my survey of the critical areas of the Comprehensive Plan with the broader Christian community. The two goals of the Plan that pertain to this area are:

> within the next decade Calvin will be recognized by the broader (multicultural) Christian community both as a credible witness of the culturally diverse character of the kingdom of God and as a leader in the development of this kingdom.

> within the next decade the college will develop a bridge of communication with the ethnic minority communities of Western Michigan that will allow for mutually beneficial interaction and genuine cooperation.[7]

As I examine the first goal, it seems to me that the broader Christian community does not usually recognize us as a credible witness of the diverse character of the kingdom of God or as a leader in its development. It is true that many noticed our efforts when we adopted the Comprehensive Plan. Abraham Davis, for example, mentioned Calvin's Comprehensive Plan when reviewing the curricular efforts of three Christian colleges.[8] But over the past ten years many have questioned the credibility of our witness and our leadership at specific times, such as when we continued to extend an invitation to Charles Murray to lecture on campus even after his controversial book, *The Bell Curve*, appeared.

Ultimately, such recognition should be earned in a way appropriate for an academic community: by means of its scholarship. At our best, the broader Christian community recognizes Calvin College as a center of productive

---

[6]*Handbook for Teaching Faculty* (Grand Rapids: Calvin College, 1995).
[7]Comprehensive Plan, 22.
[8]Abraham Davis, "Multiculturalizing the Curricula at Evangelical Christian Colleges," in *Ethnic-minorities and Evangelical Christian Colleges*, ed. D. J. Lee (Lanham, Md.: University Press of America, 1991), 291-314.

Christian scholarship in diverse areas. Unfortunately, our accomplishments in scholarship related to diversity, multiculturalism, ethnic studies, and the like are very modest. We should be leading the way in offering a Christian assessment of multiculturalism within its charged postmodern context. Although there was not a single Calvin contribution to the recent discussion of multiculturalism in the *Christian Scholar's Review*,[9] hopefully the papers of this symposium are an indication that our near silence is now over.

I do believe, however, that we are accomplishing more with respect to the second of these goal statements. Although momentum has been slow in building, two recent efforts deserve mention. First, as Director of the Multicultural Year, Chris Overvoorde has built many bridges to various communities. If you have saved the monthly calendars of the Multicultural Year and scan their back panels, you will note in the various planning committees the names of community leaders of each of the eight focus groups. The beauty of the Multicultural Year has been that "mutually beneficial interaction" has taken place each time exhibits have been planned, events scheduled, and speakers chosen. Of course, we now face a most significant challenge: Will Calvin continue in these mutually beneficial relationships, or will we fail to call on, consult with, and work with these various leaders once the Multicultural Year has concluded?

Second, Randal Jelks and I began meeting with central-city pastors more than two years ago. Those meetings have resulted in a Kellogg Foundation grant of over $600,000 that we share with twelve churches. Although some of these churches are Christian Reformed—longtime supporters of the college—others represent different traditions, both confessionally and ethnically. Included in this group are these predominantly African American churches: New Hope Baptist, True Light Baptist, and Messiah Baptist of Grand Rapids; and Holy Trinity Church of God in Christ and Great Joy World Outreach of Muskegon. What has drawn these groups together is our mutual interest in urban children and adolescents, and we have agreed to cooperate to supplement the education they receive from their neighborhood schools and to help them discover the possibilities college has to offer. Such a venture represents "mutually beneficial interaction and genuine cooperation." But this work, too, includes a challenge: What will happen after the three-year grant period?

Allow me to conclude this section with a question posed and answered by minority social scientist Henry Allen, a former Calvin faculty member:

> What should or can be done to modify the institution's cultural and racial ethos from an ethnocentric one to a more pluralistic one? First of all, the evangelical college must devote itself to establishing a constituent relationship with minority communities

---

[9]Caroline J. Simon and Bobby Fong, eds., "Theme Issue: Christianity and Multiculturalism," *Christian Scholar's Review*, June 1996: 391-507.

as a crucial priority. Therefore, college officials must seek and develop a functional and reciprocal relationship with minority communities as a crucial priority.[10]

Curriculum

The curricular goal of the Comprehensive Plan is:

> students graduating from Calvin will know and appreciate cultures other than those which are dominant in Western Europe and North America. Graduating students from all cultures will be prepared to interact effectively with people from cultures other than their own.[11]

We have been successful in many areas related to this goal of the Comprehensive Plan. The following are especially noteworthy: (1) The Science Division came out with the report, *The Development of Inclusive Courses in the Science Division,* which contains five specific recommendations for diversifying science curricula;[12] (2) As of 1985, we had only one "semester abroad" program. Now, in addition to that semester in Spain, we have programs in London, Hungary, Honduras, and New Mexico; (3) The interim term continues to provide ample opportunity for trying out new courses involving cross-cultural experience, of which many faculty and students are taking advantage; (4) In his report to the Multicultural Affairs Committee, former provost Van Harn noted curricular changes in fifteen departments in service of this goal.

In that same report, however, Dr. Van Harn also raised an important issue when he noted that "there is growing ambiguity about the goals of the college regarding diversity. The goal of studying other cultures can be interpreted broadly (international) or narrowly (North American minority)."[13] Given the more specific mandate of the Comprehensive Plan to concentrate on the latter—that is, our own backyard—such ambiguity calls for clarification, lest we neglect our neighborhood.

Despite the positive curricular growth we have seen, we still may not be meeting our goal for all of our students. Because of our previous inability to agree on goals and structure for revising the core curriculum, the relative plethora of curricular options available to our students lacks a crucial ingredient: identification of cross-cultural or multicultural values, knowledge, or skills that we require for a Calvin education. Here our cafeteria-style

---

[10]Henry Allen, "Racial Minorities and Evangelical Colleges: Thoughts and Reflections of a Minority Social Scientist," in *Ethnic-minorities and Evangelical Christian Colleges,* 145-58.
[11]Comprehensive Plan, 23.
[12]Science Division Executive Committee, *The Development of Inclusive Courses in the Science Division* (Grand Rapids: Calvin College, 1995).
[13]Gordon Van Harn, personal communication, 6 March 1996.

approach to multicultural education—take anything you want, as much as you want, or nothing at all—unfortunately mirrors certain postmodern tendencies we hope to avoid. I believe, however, that the current curriculum reform efforts at Calvin will determine how, by means of core requirements, we can implement the goal that our graduates are competent and "prepared to interact effectively with people from cultures other than their own."

Students

The goals in this area of the Comprehensive Plan focus first on the recruitment and retention of ethnic minority students—namely, that

> by 1993-94 ten percent of Calvin's student body will be comprised of ethnic minority students. By 2003-04 fifteen percent of the student body will be comprised of ethnic minority students.
>
> retention figures for ethnic minority students will not be significantly different from those of the entire student body.[14]

The goals focus second on the student body as a whole, with the goal

> that all students, from both majority and minority groups, will recognize Calvin as a genuinely multicultural community.[15]

If we look at the first goal statement, it is evident that we have fallen far shy of it. In his report to the Multicultural Affairs Committee, Vice President Thomas McWhertor reviewed the numbers: AHANA enrollment (African American, Hispanic, Asian American, and Native American) in 1985, the last year before the Comprehensive Plan, was 1.6 per cent of the student body. In 1995, the tenth enrollment year after the adoption of the plan, AHANA students comprised 3.5 per cent of the student body. The peak AHANA enrollment was 4 per cent in 1991.[16] We have not accomplished what we set out to do, either by way of enrollment or retention.

Our accomplishments with respect to the last goal—the cross-cultural sensitivity of the student body as a whole—are also modest. Consider the results from the Recent Graduates Survey, completed over the years by the Social Research Center. When asked, "During your time at Calvin (including your experiences both within and outside the classroom), how much growth did you experience in understanding cultures different from [your] own," 66.8% of the students in 1986-87 said "some or a great deal of growth," while

---

[14]Comprehensive Plan, 18.
[15]Ibid., 20.
[16]Thomas McWhertor, personal communication, 19 March 1996.

in 1994-95 only a similar 66.2% responded "some or a great deal of growth."[17]

I believe, however, that some students do encounter glimpses of what a genuinely multicultural academic community is like by means of their Calvin education. For example, when I saw a great number of Mosaic Community students this past year enter Rangeela en masse and sit in the front rows of the Fine Arts Center so as to encourage other students, I think that they were at that moment that genuine community, along with the faculty and staff who were also well-represented at this event.[18]

On a related note, consider the Mosaic Community. Made possible by a grant from the Michigan Department of Education, endorsed by the Faculty Senate, and given the leadership of Residence Life and the involvement of faculty, the Mosaic Community is a living-learning community where approximately seventy students of all backgrounds and cultures not only live together on one dorm floor but also learn together by means of a seminar and other informal learning experiences.[19] An intentional living-learning community such as the Mosaic Community is a much more effective vehicle of multicultural encounter than mere cross-cultural sensitivity sessions in orientation and/or special-focus activities in various residence halls. The shortcoming is that we cannot replicate this living-learning environment and its diverse group of students in every residence hall on campus.

Even the many activities of the Multicultural Year cannot compare in effect with a Mosaic Community. Regrettably, one student gave this assessment of student participation in the Multicultural Year: "Most students would agree that the Multicultural Year is a good thing. I don't think many students would say it's bad. But I don't think enough people are actually seeking out the events and really wanting to know the ethnic groups that are being introduced."[20] We should not conclude that the Multicultural Year has failed to influence students, but most students experienced far less of it than they could have. We should also recognize, however, that a similar assessment could be made with respect to most cocurricular campus activities. In contrast to the curriculum and to membership in the Mosaic Community, the cafeteria-style approach to multicultural encounter is often the only method available for student life.

Yet, we must hold all divisions of the college accountable for these goals. Whereas the number of ethnic minority faculty hired by the college has been

---

[17]Social Research Center, *Recent Graduates Survey* (Grand Rapids: Calvin College, 1996).

[18]Rangeela, which comes from a Hindi word meaning "the colorful," is an annual event of cultural arts sponsored and presented by Calvin's international students.

[19]See Multicultural Affairs Committee, *Background Description of the Mosaic Community* (Grand Rapids: Calvin College, 1996).

[20]Sangeetha Kumar, "Multicultural Year: One Painting in the Studio," *Dialogue*, (November/December 1996): 14.

encouraging, only two residence directors in the past ten years have been ethnic minorities, and only one admissions counselor position—other than the Multicultural Admissions Counselor slot—has been held by an ethnic minority person. Certainly, these entry-level positions with frequent turnover could provide additional opportunities for the cocurricular dimension of the college to contribute to a genuinely multicultural community.

In summary, this section of the Comprehensive Plan appears to focus on two functions of the college: admissions recruitment and student development. But we are mistaken if, in assessing our progress in these areas, we look only at numbers and programs, for the goals of this section also relate to educational climate, a point underscored by Alvaro Nieves from Wheaton, who comments:

> It is important to consider not only increasing numerical diversity, but also altering the climate within which such diversity exists. Enhancing diversity, promoting pluralism or enriching the multicultural experiences of our students is imperative if we are to equip students for participation in the modern world.[21]

Faculty

The Comprehensive Plan's goals for faculty focus on both faculty recruitment and retention. Each of these areas deserves a separate analysis.

How successful are we at *recruiting* ethnic-minority faculty? How well have we used the strategies available to us? Let me first assess our use of four strategies that are laid out in the Calvin College *Handbook for Teaching Faculty*, all of which predate the Comprehensive Plan, and some of which are expanded on in that plan. The first strategy, a strategy that we might refer to in shorthand as *hiring whether or not an opening exists*, has been used four times since it became policy in 1979. Its corresponding principle of implementation suggests why this strategy has been infrequently used: Even though a person may be hired without benefit of an opening, that person automatically moves into the next vacated position within said department. While a minority person might be eagerly accepted into a department without benefit of an opening, that person's area of expertise might not match departmental need when the next opening occurs. The bottom line: We care much and invest more in filling specific departmental needs. The dynamic inherent in this strategy suggests that we need to be greater risk-takers than our comfort levels allow in finding the right mix of personnel and academic foci within our departments. While I am not advocating that we throw out our well-planned projections for departmental staffing, I would like to suggest that we focus more on the first suggestion of this strategy that encourages us

---

[21]Alvaro Nieves, "The Minority Experience in Evangelical Colleges," *Ethnic-minorities and Evangelical Christian Colleges,* 47-64.

to "engage in a serious and *continuing* search for minority faculty members (emphasis mine)."[22]

The second strategy, that of *ensuring* that any search includes *specific efforts* to find ethnic minority candidates, is also found in the Comprehensive Plan. But in his report to the Multicultural Affairs Committee, Dean Frank Roberts suggested that this strategy has, in recent years, become pro forma. He finds that most departments have the desire to appoint minority faculty, but do not exactly know how to conduct such a search and/or are suffering from burnout in their unsuccessful searches.[23] I believe that this strategy, although cast in the spirit of the continuing search suggestion offered in the previous strategy, has not been effective due to Dean Roberts' explanation, as well as to other reasons that I relate below.

The third strategy, that of faculty exchanges, has not been operative in recent years. Although the Multicultural Lectureship in its early days brought notable lecturers to campus for a full year, a combination of budget cuts and trying to achieve more value for the expense has changed the nature of that lectureship. There are, however, ways to accomplish exchanges beyond the lectureship format. The Multicultural Affairs Committee, for example, has been working toward developing a sister-college relationship with Knoxville College, a historically black Presbyterian college. But the viability of Knoxville is in question as they face significant financial hurdles. If this relationship eventually bears fruit, such exchanges may be possible. There are, nonetheless, many opportunities for faculty exchange—if we are willing to go beyond our comfort zones.

The fourth strategy outlined in the *Handbook* also made its way into the Comprehensive Plan: the minority graduate fellowship program. This program allows a department to identify ethnic minority persons with promise for academic careers and invite them to pursue doctoral studies with financial support from Calvin. In return, they are required to teach at Calvin, at minimum, the number of years that they received support. Of the five who have entered this program, three discontinued, one is here, and another arrives this summer. It is not magnificent progress, but the program's theory is sound: Today's students can and should become tomorrow's faculty. All students should be aware that the history of the Calvin College faculty includes person after person who was encouraged to return after graduate study. This program makes that encouragement tangible.

Having looked at the use of recruitment strategy for minority faculty, we now look at its results. One of the numerical goals of the Comprehensive Plan in gathering a more diverse faculty stated that

---

[22]*Handbook for Teaching Faculty*, 218.
[23]Frank Roberts, personal communication, 26 December 1995.

by 1993-94 there will be twenty full-time ethnic minority faculty members teaching at Calvin, ten of whom will be in tenure-track positions.[24]

Rather than going back to 1993-94, let me assess this goal with respect to the current academic year of 1996-97. Both in 1995-96 and 1996-97 there have been thirteen full-time ethnic minority faculty members at Calvin. This year, nine of the thirteen are in tenure-track positions. These numbers represent a mixed picture of accomplishment. While thirteen is only 65 per cent of the goal set for 1993-94, the percent in tenure-track positions, at 90 per cent, is encouraging. But guidelines for interpretation are needed. Since the key number is small, we must guard against premature conclusions about success or failure, as one year can change the picture entirely. For example, three minority persons currently in tenure-track positions will have left by the conclusion of the 1996-97 academic year. Moreover, we can quickly offer valid reasons for this modest progress. We all know how difficult it is to find ethnic minority candidates when the number receiving Ph.D.'s in certain fields is much lower than demand.

Before we probe deeper into issues concerning minority faculty recruitment, we must look briefly at *retention*. The number of ethnic minority faculty appointed since the adoption of the Comprehensive Plan stands at twenty-eight. Today only thirteen—less than half—remain. Of the fifteen who have left, seven were tenure-track appointees and eight were term appointees. While the departure of term appointees is anticipated, the departure of seven tenure-track appointees over the last ten years, together with three more this year, means that only six of sixteen, or 38 per cent of our tenure-track ethnic minority faculty stay.

The Multicultural Affairs Committee has attempted to find answers for this low retention rate through follow-up interviews with those who have departed. Again, with such a small number any reasons given should be carefully considered but not necessarily generalized to the group as a whole since we know that the reasons for individual departure are as varied as the individuals. But these interviews corroborate a particular Achilles' heel in Calvin's ability to retain minority faculty, an area of vulnerability also identified in the Comprehensive Plan: "Experience shows two college policies that have caused problems for ethnic minority faculty are the required membership in the Christian Reformed Church and the required attendance of faculty children at Christian schools."[25]

In the recent revision and reendorsement of these policies, the authors of the document *Clarification of Calvin College Faculty Membership Requirements and Procedures for Requesting Exemptions* are also aware that such faculty requirements are "seen as a barrier to achieving ethnic and racial

---

[24]Comprehensive Plan, 9.
[25]Ibid., 12.

diversity within the faculty." Yet, they demur: "Given the high quality of our faculty, the claim of the membership requirements as a barrier to quality is dubious. Although they could be a barrier to recruiting and retaining ethnic minority faculty, Calvin's record is not significantly different from many comparable colleges."[26] Whereas the authors of the Comprehensive Plan state that these requirements are a problem, the authors of this more recent statement suggest that they are not a significant hindrance.

It is not unusual to find disagreements about how a Christian perspective should translate into personal or institutional behavior. Even the early Church struggled with this in the search for faithful and rational consistency. Paul's letter to the Galatians, for example, was largely occasioned by such a disagreement: the insistence of Jewish Christians that Gentile converts follow certain Old Testament practices. Paul's approach to this conflict is instructive for us today: He identified for the Christians in Galatia what was essential to the Gospel, what was determinative for Christian doctrine and life.

We, too, must be settled about what is essential—the essential nature of this institution and what it means to serve as a faculty member here. I trust we agree that faculty at Calvin College must teach, pursue a scholarly agenda, and serve from a Reformed perspective. In other words, our faculty must hold a Reformed worldview. Once having identified that which is essential to Calvin College, we then need to ask whether our faculty requirements—specifically those that require faculty to be members of a church in one of eight Reformed denominations and to send their children to Christian schools—are actions that are *necessary components* of a Reformed perspective or actions that are *frequent outcomes* of a Reformed perspective.

Think of this analogy. Is using cloth diapers a necessary condition of being a true environmentalist? Or is using cloth diapers a frequent outcome of an environmentalist perspective? If it is the former, then the issue is clear; there is no ambiguity. If it is the latter, we leave room for differences of opinion, choice, and a broader view of who may be considered an environmentalist—that is, the door is left open for a person to throw a box of Pampers in the grocery cart and still be a bona fide environmentalist (perhaps they consider a greater evil the earth-unfriendly reliance on fossil fuels that cloth-diaper services require).

Please do not allow the earthy nature of the analogy to distract you from the point. We at Calvin have largely held the belief that membership in certain denominations and sending one's children to Christian schools are *necessary conditions* of holding a Reformed perspective. But the other approach—to consider these actions as *frequent outcomes* of a Reformed perspective—provides room for differences in opinion and practice. It is a question of what is essential. Many, however, will probably view the latter as a slippery slope, risking the eventual loss of Calvin's Reformed identity.

---

[26] *Clarification of Calvin College Faculty Membership Requirements and Procedures for Requesting Exemptions* (Grand Rapids: Calvin College, 1995), 2.

To this objection, or fear, allow me two brief observations. First, consider the words of Abraham Kuyper from his Stone Lectures on Calvinism delivered at the turn of the century:

> The domain of Calvinism is indeed far broader than the narrow confessional interpretation would lead us to suppose. The aversion to naming the Church after a man gave rise to the fact, that though in France the Protestants were called "Huguenots," in the Netherlands "Beggars," in Great Britain "Puritans" and "Presbyterians," and in North America "Pilgrim Fathers," yet all these products of the Reformation which on your Continent and ours bore the special Reformed type, were of Calvinistic origin. But the extent of the Calvinistic domain should not be limited to these purer revelations.[27]

Second, recall that at any given time, we set aside these requirements for five to ten percent of our faculty—namely, those on one-or-two year term appointments.

In the quest to recruit and retain ethnic-minority faculty, let me venture three possible modifications to our present system of faculty requirements. First, since we already set aside the requirement for term appointments, we could set aside the requirement for any ethnic-minority faculty member. Just as we recognize that it is nearly impossible to expect a one-year term person to meet such requirements, we could do the same for ethnic-minority faculty. Let me immediately add, however, that I personally dislike this solution, for it creates something of a caste system within the faculty, not unlike the caste system that term and tenure-track appointments create.

Second, we currently rely on the Christian Reformed Church to identify "allowable denominations" by virtue of its ecclesiastical fellowships. We could abandon the church's system of determination and instead create our own list. It might be a more welcoming and inclusive list, a list that allows for a broader definition of "Reformed." But let me also add that in either instance using a denominational or ecclesiastical criterion diverts the issue from the individual where the ultimate onus and decision should rest.

That is the heart of my third possible modification. *Each* faculty member ought to initially and repeatedly "prove" to the college—the college owned and operated by the Christian Reformed Church—that he or she teaches, pursues a scholarly agenda, and serves from a Reformed perspective and that his or her doctrine or life in no way compromises the integrity of his or her Reformed witness. Included in one's "defense" might be many things: how I spend my money, how I bring justice to those who are oppressed, how I meet my civic responsibilities, and, as you might expect, how I have chosen to become a member of and participate in a local congregation and how I have chosen the school my children attend.

---

[27] Abraham Kuyper, *Calvinism* (New York: Revell, 1899), 10-11.

You see, if we are truly concerned about *outcomes* of our theology, a greater threat to the integrity of the college is the failure to monitor our own uncritical assimilation into this contemporary culture of affluence. Living out a transformational vision should impact where and how we worship on Sunday, but it should also influence where we live, how we spend our income, and how we maintain a prophetic voice in today's society.

This approach would require us to set aside the ecclesiastical charts and define what Reformed really means in the context of Calvin College. This task would require much discernment, including that of sorting through what of the college's tradition is cultural and sociological and what is theological. This approach would move the burden of proof from a small group of individuals seeking exceptions and place it on all. It would provide those who are members of the Christian Reformed Church and who send their children to Christian schools an opportunity to defend their actions as outcomes of a Reformed perspective; and it would provide those who are members of churches in other denominations and who send their children to public schools an opportunity to defend their actions as outcomes of a Reformed perspective. The latter, as well as the former, is defensible. The key is the defense.

There are, no doubt, shortcomings of this approach. For example, would it give an unfair advantage to those who are best able to make their case? Would those on the Professional Status Committee or some similar faculty-board committee fail to find the courage to point out glaring or subtle problems when faculty members' Reformed witness, critique, or voice was compromised by their affluent lifestyle, lack of active participation in the life, worship, or activities of their church, or by some other action? Would such a committee simply become legalistic and arbitrary? Or would it be simply unable to give sufficient time to a very lengthy and time-consuming process?

Searching for Causation

The Professional Status Committee and the Multicultural Affairs Committee must continue to work on the faculty-requirement issue, as well as all the other issues relative to the Comprehensive Plan. Yet it is profitable to conclude by asking why our accomplishments in respect to the Comprehensive Plan are so meager and modest.

We could focus the blame on the faculty-requirement issues, the shortage of ethnic minority Ph.D. candidates, or Calvin's ethnocentrism. We could even perhaps identify a certain faculty apathy or ambivalence toward Calvin's multicultural goals, as is suggested by John Lee and Rodger Rice when they write: "It is our impression that most people at Calvin perceive the Comprehensive Plan as having little to do with them."[28]

---

[28] J. D. Lee and Rodger Rice, "Ethnic Identity and Multiculturalism: Concepts, History, Research, and Policy," *Ethnic-minorities and Evangelical Christian Colleges*, 125.

While it is true that all of these issues contribute significantly to our lack of accomplishment, we should also not underestimate the issues of timing and context. It is unfortunate that soon after the adoption of the Comprehensive Plan "political correctness" began to sweep across the campuses of higher education, a mood that has negatively impacted Christian colleges, Calvin notwithstanding.

But we should remind ourselves that the Comprehensive Plan was not born out of any postmodern desire to be liberally inclusive or uncritically accepting; it developed rather from a Biblical vision and mandate.[29] Yet this postmodern pluralist mood has been a constant uninvited companion to all of the goals of the Comprehensive Plan, and it may very well be the source of much of our ambivalence toward them. This is a textbook example of a double bind: We wish to pursue the establishment of a genuinely multicultural academic community while rejecting the relativist leanings inherent in much postmodern thought. This is a tough image to sell when it is the postmodern impulse that largely defines what our society understands as multiculturalism.

Whether or not we conclude that our unacceptable level of accomplishment is a result of a paralysis induced by our rejection of left wing postmodernism, that context is real and our timing could not have been worse. But consider this alternative: What if the Comprehensive Plan had developed last year out of the impulse toward racial reconciliation that is being felt through much of the evangelical world?

This problem of the postmodern context, however, is our greatest opportunity. We must define what it truly means to be Christian and multicultural in a world that tends to understand something different by the term *multicultural*. Remember, arriving at a distinctly Christian critique, analysis, and understanding of a given phenomenon is a challenge we accept and strive to meet in every department on campus. We should do no less in this area and, in the process, not hide from the other contributing issues that I have identified, as well as those I have failed to mention. We should keep the Comprehensive Plan before us and strive to go beyond it.

For our multicultural project, the Calvin College Expanded Statement of Mission provides a fitting biblical vision and "uncompromising challenge," and I conclude with the latter:

> We cannot rest upon the legacy of the past. We find there, instead, places to stand from which we initiate new ventures and new partnerships. The spirit of this mission statement, then, is to employ such new partnerships and ventures in avenues of continued kingdom service.

---

[29] See Comprehensive Plan, 5.

We commit ourselves to doing even better those things that we are doing well. We seek a more vital educational program, one that meets in our studies the challenges of understanding and addressing the pressing needs of our time. We seek truly outstanding art and scholarship, in which Calvin College becomes a directing leader in forming and engaging the Christian mind. We seek partnerships in community that are more than mere relationships, but become means to transform society itself, to let justice roll down like rivers, to redress sin and wrongdoing, to further, in all instances, the kingdom of God until Christ returns.[30]

---

[30]*An Expanded Statement of the Mission of Calvin College: Vision, Purpose, Commitment*, Van Harn Commemorative Edition (Grand Rapids: Calvin College, 1996), 59-60.

The Importance of Being Earnest: A Response to Steven R. Timmermans

Michelle R. Loyd-Paige

WHEN I RECEIVED the invitation to respond to Steven Timmermans' essay, "The Comprehensive Plan: What Have We Accomplished?" I was both pleased and somewhat apprehensive. I was pleased because Calvin was choosing to celebrate its Comprehensive Plan. In a day when many major institutions within our society are rethinking their commitments to affirmative action, Calvin is not backing down from its plan to transform its campus into a more racially inclusive college so as to more accurately reflect the diversity within God's creation.

The rationale for this Multicultural Year and symposium is admirable: to bring renewed attention to the goals of the Comprehensive Plan and to strive for recommitment to them.[1] But for all my admiration, I am still somewhat apprehensive. I am apprehensive because all too often symposiums like these produce little more than a volume of papers, an exchange of lofty theoretical perspectives, and a week's worth of interesting "coffee-break talk," and I want so much more from this symposium. I want that renewed attention. I want that recommitment. I want results.

You see, for me this is personal. As many of you sit here wondering what having more of *them* on campus will mean for Calvin's identity, I am curious as to how *not having* more people who look like me on campus will affect my identity. As many of you sit here pondering what will happen to our curriculum if we integrate *their* voices and ways, I am asking, "How long will the voice of my people be silenced?" If this symposium does not seek to make a real difference; if it does not do anything other than produce a volume of papers, then let me know now because I have other things that I would rather do on a Saturday afternoon. I have a family wanting to spend time with me, and I have an intercessory prayer meeting at my home church where we storm the gates of hell. So, if all of this is just an intellectual exercise, please tell me now, and I will be on my way home. But if we are really serious, then let us work to make the goals of the Comprehensive Plan a reality. Let us make the achievement of these goals a priority.

Now, allow me to proceed to the task at hand and respond to Steven Timmermans. Overall, I appreciated his paper. I found it refreshingly practical and honest. My comments do not offer a differing perspective; instead, they serve as a kind of addendum, a commentary more practical than theoretical, more personal than abstract, and more intuitive than empirical. Timmermans addressed four critical areas of concern: the broader Christian

---

[1] Multicultural Affairs Committee, *Designation of Academic Year 1996-97 as a Multicultural Year* (Grand Rapids: Calvin College, 1996), 1.

community, curriculum, students, and faculty. My comments will also address each of these areas in the same order.

The Broader Christian Community. Here I want to raise the issue of being a credible witness. Being a credible witness is more than just doing what is right, or doing what one has a right to do. Being a credible witness also means not providing an opportunity for offense. If the exercise of our Christian or academic liberty causes someone to stumble or doubt his or her worth, then our witness becomes unfavorable in spite of all the so-called good we do. Charles Murray's visit on campus is a good example of how members of our community, minority and majority alike, were offended through the exercise of our academic liberty.

Until Charles Murray came to campus it seemed to me that everyone in my hometown of Muskegon assumed that I worked at more-neighboring Grand Valley University (no one could or would imagine I worked at Calvin). However, when the news got out that Charles Murray was coming to campus, even people I did not know would stop me and say, "Don't you work at Calvin? . . . How can you work there?" Calvin's witness was tarnished by this association, especially in the minority community. My witness was even questioned because I worked at Calvin.

Presenting Calvin College as a "good" place for minorities has not always been easy. I can remember speaking with one prominent church leader about Calvin. His impression of Calvin was that it was a Dutch school, run by the same Dutch people who built the slave ships. The appearance of Charles Murray did not help to change this man's opinion of Calvin College. For all the good the college does within and for the larger community, it takes only one incident, such as the Murray affair, to cause offense and to undo any perceived progress in race relations.

Curriculum. I understand that one of the curricular goals of the Comprehensive Plan is that "students graduating from Calvin will know and appreciate cultures other than those which are dominant in Western Europe and North America."[2] However, I question the sincerity of our pursuit of this goal. Now understand that I am a sociologist and that my opinion on this issue may be biased, but if we at Calvin are really serious about this, then why have we cut back proportionately on the number of social science courses required for core? Why must students choose between sociology or psychology? If we really wanted to be sure that our students know and appreciate other cultures, should we not require more social science courses than less? Is it not within the social sciences, especially the discipline of sociology, that students learn about other cultures?

We cannot simply count on service-learning opportunities to bridge the gap between student knowledge of other cultures and course requirements. If

---

[2]Minority Concerns Task Force, *The Comprehensive Plan for Integrating North American Ethnic Minority Persons and Their Interests into Every Facet of Calvin's Institutional Life* (Grand Rapids: Calvin College, 1985), 23.

this is not a requirement, few students will have room enough in their schedule, or energy enough, to seek out a course or experience beyond their major that will enhance their cultural understanding. We need to seriously consider the message that we are sending our students regarding cultural knowledge and appreciation. We need to be sure that our actions coincide with our words.

Students. I am sure it is not a surprise to anyone that we have not achieved our goal for AHANA student enrollment. Our progress is this area is painfully slow. While I am concerned about our numbers, I am more concerned about campus climate. By climate, I mean a *feeling of belonging* by AHANA students; I mean feelings of acceptance rather than mere tolerance of AHANA students, both individually and corporately. My observations and experience tell me that AHANA students are more tolerated than accepted. When you are tolerated rather than accepted, you get tired of defending your brand of faith. When you are tolerated rather than accepted, you grow weary of the almost daily reminders that you are here only because of some multicultural thing Calvin is trying to do—be it through scholarships, the Entrada program, or some special recruitment effort. When you are tolerated rather than accepted, you become increasingly aware of the subtle forms of racism that the dominant culture on campus either says does not exist or is oblivious to.

Faculty. As a minority faculty member, I can hardly wait for the day when I no longer represent 100 per cent of the tenured black faculty, 50 percent of the black female faculty, and 25 per cent of the total black faculty. I welcome that day for several reasons, one of which, I relate a bit tongue-in-cheek, is so that I can share with others all those wonderful lunch invitations I receive. I would love to think that I am invited to sit at the Calvin-sponsored corporate lunch tables at the various community functions because I am such an excellent scholar and teacher—because I am an excellent Calvin representative. However, I generally believe it is because I bring "color" to the table (as do Randal and Rhae-Ann). To put it rather coarsely, I am good for the multicultural image. What better way to prove that we celebrate diversity at Calvin and that our Comprehensive Plan is working than to have color at our tables? The only problem is that most people are not aware that I do not merely *represent* diversity, *I am the diversity* at Calvin, virtually, along with a few precious others!

More seriously, I am deeply concerned about the tenure requirements for faculty—specifically, the requirements of church membership and Christian school attendance by children of faculty. Having recently made it through the tenure process with a double exemption, I am concerned that my case is so unique (an ordained African American female in the Church of the Living God, CWFF, married to a public school administrator committed to public education) that I have made it harder for those who come after me to obtain an exemption. What I mean is that if the standard for the church membership exemption is previous ordination in another denomination, how many black,

Asian, Latina, or Native American women do you know who are ordained, have a Ph.D., and would want to work at Calvin? Yes, I am one of these, but there are not many like me, and I hope that I have not raised the bar so high that others are unable to cross over.

And while I am in this neighborhood, I wonder about the message we are sending to our urban partner churches. How far does the partnership go? Does it mean that we accept their kids and their faith traditions? Or do we only accept the kids? What if a member of Holy Trinity Church of God in Christ or New Hope Baptist Church (neither of which church is in ecclesiastical fellowship with the CRC) had a Ph.D. but was not ordained? Would their church membership be an issue? If it would, are we not in effect saying to our partner churches that we want your kids, but we don't want you? Give us your kids, but you adults are too deeply ingrained in your faith traditions; you are not Reformed enough to be one with us. I am not sure that we have really examined this issue enough. If we have not, we should, and soon, for our integrity and credible witness are at stake.

And finally, I ask the question, "Does one have to be Reformed, ecclesiastically, in order to have a Reformed perspective?" I do not believe so. I believe that one can have a Reformed perspective without being formally Reformed. This is the position in which I find myself. I applaud Timmermans' third option for modifying our present system of faculty tenure requirements: moving the focus away from the denomination and directing it to the individual. I think that all faculty members should be required to prove or show evidence of a Reformed perspective.

I sometimes feel that I integrate more of a Reformed perspective into my life and teaching than some of my denominational brothers and sisters here on campus. There is almost an assumption here that if you are officially Reformed, then you have a Reformed perspective, and therefore don't have to prove it. And there is almost a corresponding assumption that if you are not denominationally Reformed, the faith tradition that you do represent will dilute Calvin's Reformed identity. Being denominationally Reformed brings with it the luxury of automatic acceptance, acceptance with little proof—save for the formal statement of faith that we all must sign, save for an essay on the integration of faith and learning that we all must occasionally write, and save that one's name is listed as a member of an acceptable church—one that is in ecclesiastical fellowship with the Christian Reformed Church. (I hear, however, a bit tongue-in-cheek, that some CRC churches are not really CRC.)

I believe that a move away from denominational affiliation toward individual qualification would strengthen Calvin's Reformed identity rather than diminish it. By such a move, we would really know what it is to be Reformed, since the emphasis would be on living life and teaching from a Reformed perspective and not on birthright. If our heart's desire is to become a multicultural campus and, at the same time, a campus that maintains a strong Reformed identity, we need to seriously ask the question, "Does one have to be Reformed to have a Reformed perspective?" and in asking this question, be able to answer it in the light of all we say that we stand for, in the light of all we say we hope to achieve, and in the light of who we want to be. I believe that the way we answer this question will determine if we are to become a vital *multicultural* campus with a Reformed perspective and identity, or whether we remain a *multiracial* campus of denominationally Reformed people. There is a difference.

Calvin's Comprehensive Plan is a wonderful document with awesome goals. My prayer is that we will not grow weary in well doing, but press on to the high objectives set before us; that we, through this process of honest self-examination, will renew our commitment to these goals; that through our renewed commitment, we will persevere until we see the fruit of our labors; and that we will grow in our understanding of what it means to embrace diversity, building on our Reformed perspective, and truly become one in Christ.

Pressing On: Some Concluding Remarks

Joel A. Carpenter

I FIND IT no enviable task to give the concluding note or "last word" to a symposium whose theme—Christian identity in a multicultural world—is no simple matter, and whose concrete working out in a place such as Calvin College is no easy process. Yet, we are at an important juncture in our quest to become the community God wants us to be, and there is plenty in these papers and responses to challenge and encourage us. We have accomplished more, perhaps, than we recognize, but we also have much unfinished business.

Our first exchange of ideas highlighted the need for personal and group transformation, whether through an emptying (*kenosis*) of the desire for security and control (Thompson's essay) or through an emptying of self-denigration and passivity (Van Dyk's response). Both of these strategies are applicable to Calvin College, since both disordered attitudes are products of our own ethnic and religious minority experience. The desire to take charge of our own communal life so as to ensure its values, survival, and propagation was inscribed, perhaps, in the college's early informal motto: *onze school voor onze kinderen* ("our school for our children"). Though understandable, even spiritually commendable for a school of our heritage, this attitude can also be dangerous, for it can easily lead to serving ourselves and ourselves alone. Much of Calvin's lack of public presence, voice, and contributions, until very recently, is also related to a second liability of an immigrant community: an inferiority complex, a shame at being different, causing us to wonder if we have what it takes to make a contribution outside our own enclave. This complex, I might add, plagues a variety of evangelical communities, not just this one.

The answer to both of these injurious dispositions comes from deep within the Reformed tradition. To the first impulse, the tribal one, we must reply, with words we all cherish, "We are not our own, but belong to our faithful Savior Jesus Christ, who has bought us with his precious blood . . . and so watches over us."[1] The preservation of God's people is God's business. So is the definition of God's people. The key question for Calvin College is one that the South African philosopher, Elaine Botha, formerly of Potchefstroom University, said is key to that institution's current struggle to be transformed after the end of apartheid. As Elaine puts it: "If we say that we are put here to serve the Kingdom of God, who, then, are 'our people'?"

To the second impulse, the "light-under-the-bushel syndrome," Leanne Van Dyk's advice is exactly right. We who are tempted to think that we are nobodies in the realm of public thought and discourse need to remember that we are a people with a God-ordained purpose: to "declare the praises of him

---

[1] Heidelberg Catechism, I, Q/A 1, paraphrased.

who called [us] out of darkness into his wonderful light" (1 Peter 2:9b).[2] I am a firm believer of the notion that if we say it, and if we do it, they will come. Many of God's people will feel their hearts strangely warmed, their minds set ablaze, when they see the Gospel in all its fullness being voiced and lived and freely given to the surrounding world. If our witness lifts God up, we will draw his people into fellowship and partnership with us.

The lessons drawn from Caesar Molebatsi's narrative of the church's role in the transformation of South Africa are of absolutely stunning relevance for us here. Caesar said that three things are needed if we would see genuine reconciliation and fellowship.

First, *confession*. We must acknowledge our sin, desire forgiveness, and depend on the Cross for cleansing. If the Southern Baptist Convention can say that it is sorry for its racism, why should it be so difficult for the Christian Reformed Church and its college to do the same?

Second, a *new hermeneutic*. We need to recognize that interpreting the Bible is no grand objective science, but that it is deeply shaped by our experience. We need to see how Christians in other situations understand the same texts we study. When the apostle Paul asks us to shine like stars in a crooked and depraved generation (Phil. 2:15), how does our reading of that text compare to that of our African American brothers and sisters? To Koreans, in the United States or in Korea? To Christians in Sri Lanka? American Reformed Christianity began with some good advice that is relevant to this point. Before the Pilgrims left Leyden and got on the boat, their pastor, John Robinson, urged them to continue to listen to God's Word and to expect something fresh to keep coming from it. "The Lord hath more truth yet," he said, "to break forth out of His holy word."[3] How will we get more truth? By seeing the Scriptures through different spectacles, by sharing perspectives with brothers and sisters whose standpoint is different from ours.

The third piece of advice from Molebatsi: hear a *new call to mission*. If we make a clean breast of our sins, and seek to learn yet more truth from the Scriptures in conversation with those whose insights challenge our own, then, Caesar says, we will see God's future differently; we will have new eyes for apprehending God's task for us. Think, for example, of the changing composition of the population of the United States, what *Newsweek* magazine called "the browning of America." Does this change mean the demise of a Christian civilization or the promise of one being born? It is a religious and demographic fact that the hottest points of religious interest, new commitment, and institution building in North America right now are in the non-Caucasian subcultures. American people of West African, Korean, Filipino, Mexican, Puerto Rican, and Central American heritage are coming to Christ in far greater proportions than are the Anglos. We often look at the

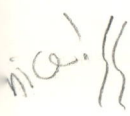

---

[2]All Scripture quotations are taken from the New International Version.
[3]Quoted in A. S. P. Woodhouse, *Puritanism and Liberty* (London: J. M. Dent, 1938), 45.

de-Christianization of Europe and shudder and wonder if that will be our fate here, too. Perhaps it will, but one of the great engines for Christian faith and its positive impact on our society has been the continuing religious searching fostered by the experience of immigration. If there is a spiritual meaning to the American experience, it is that of the sojourner, the Abrahamic impulse: "By faith he made his home in the promised land like a stranger in a foreign country; he lived in tents. . . . For he was looking forward to the city with foundations, whose architect and builder is God" (Heb. 11:9-10). The Calvin community was founded in and has been driven by this same sojourning theme, and it gives us a ready vantage point for empathizing with other pilgrims and strangers, and for seeing a new mission along with them.

There is yet more truth for us in the other presentations. David Hoekema has reminded us of the need for owning—intellectually, spiritually and morally—our multicultural aims and for discerning the difference of our understanding from that of postmodern multiculturalism. Something Hoekema pointed out for which I am particularly grateful is that we have indeed been able to accomplish some important things over the last decade in curriculum, student life, community relations, and faculty development. We need not be discouraged; God has blessed our commitment and our labors with some genuine fruit. One dramatic change, that might seem too modest to count, and which we have yet to absorb into our outlook: Calvin has opened its doors wide to students from outside the Christian Reformed Church. An astonishing change has taken place as a result in the last twenty years. Perhaps our sense of helplessness in changing campus cultural patterns and outlook is a bit overwrought.

Steven Timmermans has reminded us of the very concrete promises we have made as a community, how far we have and have not come toward making good on those promises, and what we should consider changing in order to overcome some of the obstacles we face. Timmermans has really nailed one of the key problems, especially when it comes to faculty recruitment and retention. We seem to forget that Reformed Christianity is a movement that overflows denominational boundaries. Tests of commitment to the Reformed tradition should reflect its fluidity as a movement. It is not just an ecclesiastical territory. Our Christian school requirement, which addresses a field that evokes so much passion and sacred memory in the Christian Reformed community, may do more than any other of our faculty requirements to discourage possible recruits. Faculty candidates who share all of what it means to be Reformed except for some of the most particular ministry commitments of the Christian Reformed denomination are lost to Calvin College because of this requirement. Others join us on these terms, but continue to feel the imposition of a practice that is foreign to their prior commitments as God's agents in the world. Don't get me wrong: The Christian day-school movement is a worthy and noble strategy that Christian Reformed people have adopted for witnessing to the kingdom. Yet there are other Reformed approaches and perspectives. If Calvin College wants to be a

Reformed confessional institution with a world vision and a multicultural constituency, then it should acknowledge the breadth of legitimate Reformed thought on these matters. These are my opinions on matters that are salient for faculty development. They are, of course, not the views of us all by any means. So let us continue the conversation, for this issue will not go away.

Having revealed my own mind on one issue, let me communicate the consensus of the other officers of Calvin on multicultural matters more generally. We are committed to the vision of the Comprehensive Plan. We *will* continue to work proactively to achieve, even to exceed, its various goals:

In *Admissions*. We will work harder to recognize that the key to strong and sustainable minority and international enrollments is very similar to the key to strong and sustainable Christian Reformed enrollments: building partnerships of trust and common mission with local churches and other Christian ministries. If we have such partnerships, then there will be ethnic minority religious communities that will say of Calvin: "That's our school, for our children." We have a long way to go in that regard, but we have made a start, and there shall be no turning back. It can be done! Consider a number of Christian colleges, urban institutions much like our own, and what they have been able to accomplish in minority enrollment:

Seattle Pacific University: 9.4%
Dallas Baptist University: 30.7%
Oral Roberts University 39%
North Park College 34.7%
LaSierra University: 59.5%[4]

We should be consulting with faculty and staff at these colleges to find out why they are succeeding in minority enrollment.

In *Curriculum*. We will make sure that the current review and revision of the core curriculum recognizes the absolutely critical and indispensable role of cross-cultural experience and understanding in educating our students for kingdom service. We will identify current curricular offerings, create some new ones if necessary, and present a thoughtful and flexible approach to building these into core requirements. We are also pledged to expand the opportunities to live, study, and serve in cross-cultural settings here in North America and abroad.

In *Student Life and Community Affairs*. We hope to see the Mosaic Dorm experiment expand and one day encompass the entire campus. We want the friendships and partnerships engendered in this multicultural year to last and flourish. We want every year to have features of this multicultural year. We scarcely realized how much we had been missing, right here in West Michigan. In our opportunities to learn by serving, we hope to engage with our new friends and contacts as well.

---

[4]Data reported to the Pew Younger Scholars Program, University of Notre Dame.

I see a new day dawning, in so many different dimensions, for Calvin College as a "public" institution, with a public witness, a public voice, and a sense of responsibility to a larger community. But this commitment will have to include a willingness to get out there and mix it up, to be vulnerable, and to take our lumps as well as our laurels.

It is late in the school year and we are weary. We have not met our Comprehensive Plan goals, and we are discouraged, maybe even cynical. But I hope this conference has been encouraging, and has lifted our sights. So, as the writer of the epistle to the Hebrews puts it, let us "strengthen [our] feeble arms and weak knees," as we seek to "throw off everything that hinders and the sin that so easily entangles, and let us run with perseverance the race marked out for us" (Heb. 12:12,1).

The Multicultural Year: A Retrospective

Chris Stoffel Overvoorde

INTRODUCTION

IT IS DIFFICULT to look back without amazement on this year, for so much has taken place. There were over one hundred events connected with the Multicultural Year, including: ten ethnic dinners, beginning with a multicultural smorgasbord picnic and concluding with an American style picnic; thirty-three cultural events, including plays, films, concerts, and other activities; twelve exhibitions, including four fine arts exhibitions in the Center Art Gallery; forty-four lectures and sixteen chapels, all of which provided unique opportunities to learn and discover new ways of looking at this richly diverse world. Almost fifty community people became involved in the planning process, making this Multicultural Year a very special community effort. These are the statistical facts, but they do not tell the whole story, for they cannot reflect the numerous discussions that have taken place surrounding these events, nor can they reflect the new insights that were gained during these discussions. I am sure that Calvin College is a richer place because we celebrated in a small way our diversity and unity in Christ. Below you will find a more detailed description of what has taken place this year. At the end I have made some observations and recommendations for the Multicultural Affairs Committee in its ongoing concern for Calvin's multicultural vitality.

Opening Activities

The Fall Faculty Conference was held on Tuesday, September 3, 1996. Justo González gave the keynote address in the morning, followed by workshops related to each of the cultures we were to monthly observe. These workshops were repeated before lunch. After lunch each department was asked to follow up on the conference theme in their particular departmental discussions.

A Festival of Cultures took place on September 12, 1996, on the Commons Green between 3:30 and 7:30 P.M. Food, displays, and music were part of this festival organized by the Student Activities Office under David Guthrie.

The Opening Event officially took place that night in the Fine Arts Center. Chinese martial artists performed a Lion Dance that led people from the Commons to the stage of the Fine Arts Center. The program also included: *Orquesta Creacion*, a Latino band, that played Mexican, Puerto Rican, and Cuban music; John Bailey (*Animkee*), a Native American Indian, who told a story; the Polish Heritage Choir that sang Polish folk art songs; the Korean Folklore Association that performed traditional Korean music; a Laotian Choir that sang traditional songs; the Arab American Association that presented a fashion show with traditional Arab music and dance; and songs of praise rendered by the Grand Rapids Area Choral Ensemble (GRACE). President Byker spoke words of welcome and Charsie Sawyer and Darlene Meyering hosted this fine evening in which we were all embraced by each other's rich cultural ways.

The Months

The highlight for *September*, Latino Month, was the exhibition *Faith and Hope: Art of Hispanic Culture* (*Fe Y Esperanza: Arte de Cultura de Hispano*), curated by José Narezo and Chris Stoffel Overvoorde. A reception and a lecture supported that effort. There were also some very fine speakers and the first folk art exhibition was installed in the Chapel lobby.

October, Korean American Month, will be remembered for the special visit of the Seoul Metropolitan Dance Theater as they presented traditional music and dance for us in a full Fine Arts Center. We also had chapels, lectures, and even a film evening, as well as a fine folk-art exhibit.

The highlight for *November*, Native American Month, has to be the Veterans Anishinabe Pow Wow held in the Calvin Fieldhouse. This event was well attended and the participation was excellent. Sally Thielen was one of the many speakers. Later, in January, we also featured a fine-art exhibit of this Native American artist.

December, Arab American Month, was a short month due the holidays and exams, but the Arab Community came together in the Gezon Auditorium and presented a fine evening of traditional Arab music led by the Dearborn Traditional Arabic Ensemble. The meal was also an outstanding event.

January was designated Chinese American Month, but it was dominated by the January Series and the Interim term. In some ways the many students who went off campus implemented our multicultural efforts in a very concrete way. Several lectures in the January Series were related to the Multicultural Year, such as the opening lecture by Dr. Hanan Ashrawi, Minister of Higher Education in Palestine. In the midst of all this, we celebrated Martin Luther King Week with some very fine activities. The Chinese Month concluded with a Chinese New Year's celebration in the Commons Dining Hall on February 1. The attendance was overwhelming and everyone had a great time. It must also be noted that this was the first time that the Chinese church, the Asian Center, and the Chinese American Association collaborated on such an event.

February, African American Month, was filled to the brim with activities, and it is difficult to pick one highlight, for there were many fine speakers such as Dr. Drew Smith, Dr. Houston Baker, Dr. Lerone Bennett, and Dr. James Banks, as well as the Sounds of Blackness, which almost sold out the Fine Arts Center. It was a great month.

The Tamburitzans came in *March* to help us celebrate Eastern European Month. We did not fill the Fine Arts Center, but it was one of the best events of the year in terms of fittingness and enjoyment.

The Laotian and Cambodian celebration of culture highlighted *April, Southeast Asian American Month*. It was a fine evening in the Chapel undercroft where we enjoyed great food and fellowship and, later, in the Chapel a fine program of dance, music, and images from these unique cultures.

Concluding Activities

The Multicultural Year concluded with two activities. On April 25 and 26 a symposium on multicultural issues entitled, *The One in the Many: Christian Identity in a Multicultural World,* was well attended. It included presentations by Dr. Thomas Thompson, Calvin College; Rev. Caesar Molebatsi, Director of Youth Alive Development Corporation, South Africa; Dr. Samuel Solivan, Andover Newton Seminary; Dr. David Hoekema, Calvin College; and Dr. Steven Timmermans, Calvin College. Responses were by Dr. Leanne Van Dyk, San Francisco Theological Seminary; Rev. Glandion Carney, Centrepointe Church, Grand Rapids; Dr. Richard Plantinga, Calvin College; Dr. Cornelius Plantinga Jr., Calvin College; and Dr. Michelle Loyd-Paige, Calvin College. Provost Joel Carpenter of Calvin College offered concluding remarks. Faculty, staff, board members, and students also met in three different workshops on the second day to offer recommendations to the Multicultural Affairs Committee. The Spring Arts Festival on May 1 and 2 included a concluding picnic for the students and the community. Even though the rain dampened many of the planned activities of this festival, our spirits were not dampened because we sensed that we had accomplished something truly celebrative through the Multicultural Year.

Looking Back

I look back on this last year with gratitude and joy, for it has been a most delightful experience to be involved in this kingdom-building adventure. The whole process was not unlike that of creating a painting. When you are confronted with that big white surface called a canvas, you have, at first, only a vague idea of what may happen. While you paint, things do begin to happen, and from there you seek and learn and discover in the process so that the groping turns to understanding. Initially, I had an inner conviction that the Multicultural Year's celebration was the right thing to do, that it needed to be done, but I had no way of knowing how it would all turn out or how it would be received. I can now say that this elusive thing called multiculturalism has become clearer because we experienced it; we lived it. It was the process of doing that taught us what it is and what it could be.

My main focus and contribution this year is that I have been actively working with the various ethnic communities, many of whom have never been officially connected with Calvin College. Some of these contacts have been difficult, others have been a joy and delight. When certain community leaders ask the question, "What will you do next year?" it is because they have enjoyed the contact, appreciated the results, and would like to continue to work together. As a result, it is my firm belief that we as a college will serve the community and the denomination well by retaining many of these contacts. We should continue to provide avenues of interaction with these groups—at the very least, by continuing the various venues of the multicultural year, such as lectures, exhibits, concerts, or performing activities.

Now that I have reached out in my task as director of the Multicultural Year, it is essential for Calvin College to continue to strengthen the tenuous bridges that have been built. Some of the relationships we have established are very fragile structures that need to be maintained with honesty, openness, respect, and integrity. It will take a special community-sensitive person to continue this task. I hasten to acknowledge that several people have already done, and continue to do, much of this work. Rhae-Ann Booker has reached out to several groups beyond the African American community, especially the Native American community. She and Julie DeGraw have laid the foundation for a relationship with this group. Peter Szto has worked closely with the various Asian groups, and I have built on his work. Harvey Scott has visited many churches and has made other important contacts, but these have not been fully utilized in my view. Randal Jelks has made numerous contacts and has extensive knowledge of the various academic communities. But while these persons have reached out in the context of their particular college positions and mandates, I have had no other agenda, no specified task that motivated me other than the college's interests as a whole. My task was to educate students about ethnic and cultural variety—majority student as well as minority. In a sense, I was free to move unrestricted. I believe it is essential to assign someone who knows this college well and has an interest in the larger community to continue in this role. I further believe that the slot originally intended for such community development should now be reinstated, modified, and clarified, and should function somewhat like that of the director of the Multicultural Year.

In my role as multicultural educator, I attempted to facilitate an educational experience that went beyond stereotype and academic jargon. Such community contact was a new wrinkle for Calvin College, for it did not allow us to assume that we—the academic community—were the greater source of knowledge, as is often our posture. Instead, I went to the various communities and asked what they would like to do for us. This grassroots approach resulted in a variety of educational formats, a variety of activities—sometimes a concert, sometimes a play or another performing art, many times a speaker. Perhaps not suprisingly, students and the Calvin community at large have responded in greater numbers to the performing-arts activities such as the Seoul Korean Dance Theater performance and the Anishinabe Pow Wow than to most of the lectures. The result of all these activities has been mutually educational and enriching: Not only did Calvin have many opportunities to experience elements of a particular culture but many an ethnic community had opportunity to learn something about the college.

This was possible because of a great deal of promotion and publicity, an advertising blitz united by one visual image, the flower bouquet, which I designed to symbolize the rich cultural diversity of God's good creation. Through this, our multicultural effort has become a public effort. The Comprehensive Plan, adopted ten years ago, was an internal plan that has not been publicized; neither has the multicultural statement the faculty endorsed in 1993 seen wide circulation. But this year we are no longer going quietly about our business—we are doing it in front of everyone. While the public-relations efforts for this year were especially demanding, they reaped many a dividend. But they are also a liability, for not only do they promote Calvin College's programs and efforts, they also make it possible for us to be held accountable for what we have done—*and are not doing*. It is therefore essential that we determine in this area what is important to us, what we really value, to what we are committed, and what the shape of that commitment will be. This year our multicultural efforts were very obvious, very public. Next year we will not be that public even if the same activities continue, for we will not have the concerted focus or the financial support to the degree that we had this year. Yet, if we lose that public dimension entirely, we will lose face with many of the organizations and people we have been working with. I believe that it is now essential that the multicultural activities remain intensively and purposely *public*, just like the January Series. Moreover, the January Series can function as a model, hopefully including the financial support it has gained over the years.

As the year progressed, it became apparent that we needed to begin a support system for all those involved in multicultural activities. We created the Multicultural Team. Consequently, Rhae-Ann Booker from the Multicultural Student Development Office, Brian Davis from the Mosaic Community, Randal Jelks of the Multicultural Lectureship, Jacqueline Rhodes from Academic Services, Harvey Scott from the Admissions Office, and I, began to explore additional ways in which we could cooperate and support each other. We met on a regular basis, sharing visions and goals, as well as activities. It became evident that some of us needed to reach beyond the restrictions and responsibilities defined by our various offices, that others needed a voice beyond that of a supervisor, but that all of us needed to reach out more to the college as a whole than is currently suggested and structured by the various college documents. We need to develop a structure in which we have a central office, or person, who directs the activities of all the multicultural efforts, or this could be organized through some kind of cabinet of multiculturalism.

Awareness of Calvin's multicultural goals, not just by the team, but by everyone in the college must be heightened. Communication therefore is essential. The *Mosaic Newsletter* could begin to function in this way, but I believe that other means need to be provided beyond that newsletter. All those who supervise the various college efforts also need to become more informed of and involved in the tasks of others so that, when changes are made, we, in turn, communicate clearly with those who are doing the job. The fact that we as a team frequently found ourselves in the position of asking questions indicates that something is lacking—namely, open communication and dialogue even among those who are trying to effect change. This lack of communication, however, is widespread and goes even deeper—it probably manifests a larger apathy to these issues. Those lacking concern, however, ought not think that the problem of multiculturalism goes away by appointing some minority person to some position. The issue of multiculturalism does not belong especially to them, though it may affect them the most. *No, it belongs to all of us*. Each faculty member must be committed to the goal of becoming a multicultural educational community, as has been so well stated in the document endorsed by the faculty (1993). Moreover, various faculty members need to work together with the various minority faculty and staff to become this community. I believe some kind of mentoring program for incoming faculty, both for minorities and majorities, is essential. While mentoring takes place now in departments, it should expand to include a mentoring that has a broader college scope. Minority faculty and staff need support, need a "buddy" to see them through the first years here at Calvin. And they especially need to be given an opportunity to fit according to their strengths, their beliefs, and their cultures. If it is true that we do not need to drop anything of our Dutch culture to become minority-sensitive persons, and that a multicultural campus enriches all those on the campus, why would we want to remake those who come from different cultures into that of our "peculiar North American Dutch" culture?

Summary of Observations

1. Students and the Calvin community have responded in greater numbers to the *performing-arts activities* such as the Seoul Korean Dance Theater performance and the fall Anishinabe Pow Wow than to most of the lectures.

2. It is essential that certain dimensions of our multicultural activities remain *public*. The Multicultural Year has built good bridges between the college and the community that are of great benefit in making Calvin a more diverse place. We need the community to make this possible and to maintain it. If it is possible to make some of the lectures available to the public by, for example, inviting the Korean community to join us whenever we have a Korean speaker, that would maintain the bridge building. If, for another example, we have a Chinese cultural event in the planning stage and we can invite some Chinese leaders to advise us and get their support, that event will become more successful.

3. Based on my experience with the Multicultural Team, I strongly urge the continuation of something like it in a more formal way. We need to develop a structure in which we have a central office, or person, who promotes the activities of all the multicultural efforts, or some kind of cabinet of multiculturalism.

4. Communication is essential. Awareness of our various multicultural goals, not just by the team, but by everyone in the college community, is invaluable. The *Mosaic Newsletter* could begin to function in this way, but more avenues of communication need to be provided beyond that newsletter.

5. Communication with the outside community has been good this year. I am not convinced, however, that the support we have gained from the various cultural communities has affected campus life all that much. The attendance figures were not that impressive for many events. We need to explore additional ways to reach the staff and the students. The term *multicultural* may be a hindrance in that regard, and we may need to broaden our sight and our terminology. The idea of a world arts series is very appealing, for it incorporates the international students who have become a strong voice on our campus. The work done by the Student Life Division is absolutely essential in this connection. They need to be recognized and supported, for the work they do is often less public and limited to the campus community. To gain the support for multiculturalism or internationalism from the staff and the students as well as the student organizations is very important as we plan for the future.

6. It is good to remember what we have accomplished and to restate our goals. The theme we adopted in the beginning of the year was, "That They May Be One." We have practiced this theme throughout the year with various cultures by bringing them onto our campus. While this has provided us with many opportunities to learn and to discover, we have not always prepared this community ahead of time to be good hosts to our guests. For example, we were insufficiently prepared for the Pow Wow as to its meaning and significance. We need to be involved in dialogue with each other about the religious implications of various cultural expressions and use such opportunities to educate, to reflect, and to study, so that we are informed and prepared for what is to come. In the enthusiasm of the moment, we have not always allowed this opportunity for dialogue to flourish. Our concern for learning and for creating a diverse community on this campus must remain the major focus of our efforts.

7. A diverse community on this campus cannot become a reality without the support of the church. The relationships with the Latino and the Asian communities within our denomination need to be strengthened as we look

toward the future. This past year we have been more successful at interacting with the Asian community than with the Latino community.

8. One of the first arguments I got into in this position concerned the fact that we did not include the Dutch as one of our cultures to explore. I have found that there are many on our campus who are leery about "all this multicultural stuff" for fear of losing our Dutch culture. The North American Dutch culture is a unique culture, and we do not need to apologize for it, nor do we need to lose it. This is not an either/or question, however. To become multicultural does not mean that we have to give up something, but that we can gain something. I will always be Dutch, no matter what. But being exposed to all the cultural variety this year has made me a richer person. I have made many friends, gained numerous insights, and have developed a new appreciation for others who think and act differently than I do. But I am still a Dutchman. It is as a Dutchman that I digest all that new stuff. In the same way, I challenge this community to know its roots, to know its culture and appreciate it. I think it is unfortunate that the Dutch Department is no longer a department; we will therefore need to find new ways to communicate and celebrate our own Dutch heritage.

These are my observations throughout this year, and based on these I recommend the following:

My Recommendations

1. Continue the cultural programming of the various ethnic groups throughout the year. If possible, involve the specific cultural organizations for participation and promotion. This way we will continue the effort of the Multicultural Year by establishing a Multicultural Series in the coming year. It has been suggested that we call it a world arts series, which sounds excellent to me.

2. Formalize the Multicultural Team concept into a council or cabinet so that those most directly involved in these efforts can support each other. This cabinet would report regularly to the Multicultural Affairs Committee and be a subcommittee of MAC.

3. Continue to build bridges with the various communities. They should be selected according to three criteria: are they present in or among (1) students and staff; (2) the church; and/or (3) the West Michigan area. As previously suggested, the college could support the church in this vein by concentrating its efforts on a focus group or "culture of the year."

4. Expand the mandate and scope of the *Mosaic Newsletter* to publicize more fully all of the multicultural opportunities available to our students, staff, and alumni.

5. Produce a brochure stating our commitment as a college to be a multicultural community and informing students about the many multicultural opportunities available on campus throughout the year. Currently a brochure is in production for the recruitment staff, but I am recommending that one be available for all students, faculty, and staff.

6. Continue to work with more particular cultural communities and not assume a too-generalized concept of certain groups, as we did with the Latino and the Southeast Asian cultures.

7. Continue to observe such events as the Martin Luther King celebration, black history month, and other nationally designated months.

8. Reach out to the other educational communities in support and coordination of activities. Both the area colleges and high schools are becoming more active in this area, and we at Calvin College can provide some much needed support and guidance.

9. Continue to work with the Native American peoples and have a repeat of the Anishinabe Pow Wow.

10. Continue to work with the Chinese community and see if we can repeat the Chinese New Years celebration.

11. Continue to work with the denomination and provide support and encouragement to the Office of Race Relations so that the entire denomination becomes a multicultural community.

12. Explore the possibility of establishing a mentoring program for incoming minority faculty. Currently mentoring takes place within departments, but this program should help introduce the specific Dutch American culture to the newcomer from an overall perspective rather than the narrower perspective of a given discipline.

Soli Deo Gloria

Near Heroes: A Meditation for a Multicultural Year

Thomas R. Thompson

> On one occasion an expert in the law stood up to test Jesus. "Teacher," he asked, *"what must I do to inherit eternal life?"*
> "What is written in the Law?" he replied. "How do you read it?"
> He answered: "'*Love the Lord your God with all your heart and with all your soul and with all your strength and with all your mind'; and, 'Love your neighbor as yourself.'*"
> "You have answered correctly," Jesus replied. "Do this and you will live."
> But he wanted to justify himself, so he asked Jesus, *"And who is my neighbor?"*
> In reply Jesus said: "A man was going down from Jerusalem to Jericho, when he fell into the hands of robbers. They stripped him of his clothes, beat him and went away, leaving him half dead. A priest happened to be going down the same road, and when he saw the man, he passed by on the other side. So too, a Levite, when he came to the place and saw him, passed by on the other side. But a Samaritan, as he traveled, came where the man was; and when he saw him, he took pity on him. He went to him and bandaged his wounds, pouring on oil and wine. Then he put the man on his own donkey, took him to an inn and took care of him. The next day he took out two silver coins and gave them to the innkeeper. 'Look after him,' he said, 'and when I return, I will reimburse you for any extra expense you may have.'
> "Which of these three do you think was a neighbor to the man who fell into the hands of robbers?"
> The expert in the law replied, *"The one who had mercy on him."*
> Jesus told him, "Go and do likewise."[1]

DURING THIS INTERIM term our chapels have gathered around the theme of "a great cloud of witnesses," an image found in Hebrews 12:1 in reference to the preceding chapter, eleven, which presents us with a gallery of heroic saints—people who lived distinguished lives of faith or who performed distinguished acts of faith, people whom we might call in more popular parlance, *heroes* or *sheroes* of faith. In keeping with that theme, and in view of the Multicultural Year we are now celebrating, I would like to focus our reflections on some *near heroes* of the faith.

The text before us is a familiar one: the parable of the Good Samaritan. Its message is seemingly simple and basic. A lawyer with questionable

---

[1] Luke 10:25-37. All Scripture quotations are taken from the New International Version, emphases mine.

motives (which some might argue is no oxymoron) asks Jesus no shabby, insignificant question: "What must I do to inherit eternal life?" How, in other words, can I be saved? Jesus replies by asking him a question (Jesus is, after all, Jewish): How do you interpret the Torah; what do you consider the heart of the Law, the hub upon which salvation turns? To this question the lawyer recites what was most likely a creed in the Jewish worship of the time, a combination of Deuteronomy 6:5 and Leviticus 19:18, that which we know from other texts to be the greatest commandment and its corollary: "'Love the Lord your God with all your heart and . . . soul and . . . strength and . . . mind'; and, 'Love your neighbor as yourself'" (Luke 10:27). For that answer, Jesus says to the lawyer, you receive a passing grade (remember, it's only Interim): *Do this* and you will *excel* in life.[2]

But the lawyer is not completely satisfied with this answer, for one reason or another, and so with the rigor and persistence of a Christopher Darden, a Marcia Clark, or a Johnnie Cochran, he questions Jesus once again: "And who is my neighbor?" Now, before Jesus answers him once again with a question, which he will, he relates a story, that which we have come to call the parable of the Good Samaritan (You see, Jewish people not only like to ask questions; they also are very fond of telling stories): Traveling down a dangerous road, a man whom the original hearers of the parable would understand to be Jewish fell into the hands of brigands. He was robbed, stripped naked, beaten unconscious, and left near to death. A priest of the prestigious Jewish upper class rides near and says, "Better not get involved." (After all, if the man were dead, and the priest came too close, he would become ceremonially unclean, and unable to perform his tasks as a priest. It was his *duty* to pass on.) Similarly, a Levite of a slightly lower class than the priest walks by, but also decides not to get involved. (After all, the robbers may still be around lying in wait. It simply wouldn't be *prudent* to stop.) So it falls to a Samaritan to come riding by, who, moved with compassion for this innocent victim, administers first aid, and then goes an extra mile or two to see this unknown person through to recovery.

Again, the message of the parable appears to be rather plain and simple; to the question, Who is my neighbor? the answer seems to be, anyone who is in need. And that, after all, would comport well with how James, in 1:27, defines the poles of true religion: "Religion that God our Father accepts as pure and faultless," says James, "is this: to look after orphans and widows in their distress" (which is love of neighbor, especially of the vulnerable and the

---

[2]This chapel meditation was delivered on January 22, 1997, during Calvin's January Interim term in which most classes are graded on the simple basis of pass or fail. My exegesis of this parable was greatly benefited by Kenneth E. Bailey's *Through Peasant Eyes: A Literary-Cultural Approach to the Parables of Luke* (Grand Rapids: Eerdmans, 1980), esp. 33-56, and Bastiaan Van Elderen's "Another Look at the Parable of the Good Samaritan," in *Saved by Hope: Essays in Honor of Richard C. Oudersluys*, ed. J. I. Cook, (Grand Rapids: Eerdmans, 1978), 109-19.

helpless) "and to keep oneself from being polluted by the world" (which is love of God, over and against any usurping worship of creation—note the order of presentation, however).

Now while this is a true and noble doctrine or teaching in and of itself, it is not quite the point of Jesus' parable. This can be seen in the question that Jesus immediately asks the lawyer after he relates the story of the Samaritan's compassionate act. Jesus' final question does not point to the naked and victimized man. Rather, he asks the lawyer: "Which of *these three* do you think *was a neighbor* to the man who fell into the hands of robbers? Which of these three: the Priest, the Levite, or the Samaritan?"—the answer to which does not require a Calvin College degree. And so it seems that the lawyer who came to test Jesus winds up examining himself. To his first question (and these are highlighted in the opening text before you)—what must I do to inherit eternal life?—the lawyer himself supplies the correct answer: love God and neighbor. To his second question—Who is my neighbor?—the legal expert is compelled by the way that Jesus phrases his rejoinder to answer, not the man in need, but the, and here one can imagine something like Fonzie on Happy Days attempting to say I'm wrong: the Sammm . . ., the Sammm . . ., *the one who had mercy on him.*[3]

The Samaritan, Jesus, that's my neighbor? Those half-breed sell-outs to the Assyrians? The ones who claim to be the true remnants of the Northern tribes of Israel, who set up a rival form of worship on Mt. Gerazim as the so-called keepers of the faith? Those beady-eyed, hook-nosed, onion-and-leek-reeking moochers, who are forever crossing our borders and taking away our jobs. Why, they practically own every quickie bagel shop in the province. Some even say they're behind the economic woes of the whole region. Those greedy tightwads. They're so pompous and opinionated that they think they know what's good for everyone; and they're always tripping over themselves trying to help in their paternalistic way. Why they're so tight muscled that they can't even keep a beat. And Lord knows, Samaritan men can't jump. A parable about a good Samaritan? Now there's an oxymoron for 'ya. I'll tell you what they're good for, they're good for nothing. A(rchie) Bunkerstein put it right when he said: The only good Samaritan is a dead Samaritan.

Needless to say, the antipathy between Jews and Samaritans ran deep in history, and was fueled by misunderstandings, conflicts, injustices, and even atrocities *on both sides*. This deep-seated prejudice is even manifest in Jesus' disciples, specifically James and John, the so-called Sons of Thunder, who when not welcomed in a certain Samaritan village asked Jesus, "Lord, do you want us to call fire down from heaven to destroy them?" (Luke 9:52). Jesus promptly rebuked them. Indeed, for the Jews the name "Samaritan" became a term of de*nig*ration, an ethnic slur, as is evident in John 8:48 when Jesus himself is called a Samaritan and demon-possessed in the same breath.

---

[3]Bastiaan Van Elderen, my New Testament professor at Calvin Theological Seminary, first brought this parabolic twist to my attention.

And so the lawyer did not receive from Jesus the exact answer he was looking for, the answer to his question, "And who is my neighbor?" But just what sort of answer was the legal sleuth seeking? The text tips us off: "But he wanted to justify himself, so he asked Jesus, 'And who is my neighbor?'" (10:29). The lawyer, it seems, was looking for a self-justifying answer, an answer that was self-confirming. He would prefer that Jesus list those sorts of people who were already near or nigh unto him; those people to whom he already was, in all probability, a good neighbor: family, friends, fellow countrymen. But Jesus' answer indicts at many points. Leaving aside the issue of family, our closest neighbors, whom we are already predisposed to love and to whom we quite evidently have neighborly obligations, Jesus challenges the lawyer's self-drawn neighborhood. Would the lawyer have helped his fellow countryman, the innocent Jewish victim of robbers? Perhaps. But if his friends' actions are any indication, the lawyer could very well have failed in this basic humanitarian act. You see, by using as examples the failures of the priest and the Levite, Jesus was indicting what was probably the lawyer's most immediate circle of friends and influence, the people he was most likely to associate with, the people with whom he would socially hobnob. It takes the Samaritan to cross the picket lines of family, friends, social class, and ethnic clan to shatter the boundaries of the neighborhood. Why does the Samaritan risk life and limb to draw near to the Jewish victim? Not so that he could say that he once helped a Jew, or so that his relatives could say something like, "Hey, I got an uncle who once helped a Jew." Presumably, he drew near the man because he saw in him, plainly and simply, a human person in need, naked and helpless, just like all of us are before God—naked and helpless we are born; naked and helpless we die. The priest and Levite were "near heroes," that is, nearly heroes; they came, they saw, but in the end they did not conquer their own fears or social conventions; they failed the test of love of neighbor. Only the Samaritan is the "near hero" of faith, the one who drew nigh because he recognized in the helpless man one who is near to himself, one who is, at bottom, like himself. Terence once famously wrote, "I am human; nothing human is foreign to me." Jesus offers us this modification: "*no one* human is foreign to me."

So who are *our* neighbors, the ones near us that we are to love as evidence and pursuit of life eternal? Certainly our family; certainly our friends. But let's pause for a moment on friends. It has long been observed that friendship is based on similarity and common interests. Our friends are a reflection of ourselves. Take a look at your friends and you will see your own likeness and interests. This should be a source of healthy confirmation (if I am anything like those I consider my friends, I can take some basic pride in the person that I am or want to be). But friendship can also serve to justify those interests that, though common among friends, may not be so common to the human race. Friends can more easily reinforce, justify, and confirm our own selves and our ways of life in unhealthy directions—for example, in our *self-interests*, biases, and prejudices. And friendship can easily draw a circle around itself and become simply an end in and of itself. So do we subscribe in our friendships to a higher law, one that enables friends at times to say to each other, "I don't think this is right," and yet remain friends?

While we cannot be friends with everyone (indeed, I think the label "friend" ought to be used most discriminately), we must be careful that in planning the zones of our lives we do not draw the boundaries of our neighborhoods too narrowly—merely around our family and friends, and then by extension around those most like us, whether we be white, Anglo-Saxon, Protestant; or red, yellow, or black. "If you love those who love you," says Jesus, "what credit is that to you? Even 'sinners' love those who love them. And if you do good to those who are good to you, what credit is that to you? Even 'sinners' do that" (Luke 6:32).

Christ calls us to become "near heroes" of faith, people who draw near to those who are nearer to us than we think due to the artificial impediments we create to discriminate persons and to justify our own lack of love and involvement. Who are the "near heroes" of today? Anyone who breaks these plastic barriers of social convention or convenience, whoever embraces the needy other in spite of their otherness: people such as the hospice worker, Mother Teresa, or Keshia Thomas, the eighteen-year-old African American woman, who, while protesting a Ku Klux Klan rally last June in Ann Arbor, threw herself over the body of a sheet-wearing wanabe to defend him from anti-Klan protesters turned violent. Perhaps you recall the photograph; a lesson in contrast, the Samaritan and the Jew. These are more extreme examples, and there is a spectrum of degrees of near heroes. The kingdom of God is about all of these—it is big and wide and goes to the extremes.

In one of his novels, Fyodor Dostoyevsky ruminates that such sacrificial love for one's neighbor is a miracle impossible on earth. One can love one's neighbor in the abstract, or even at a distance, but at close quarters we stumble over a smell, a face, an insult or injury given.[4] Perhaps the lawyer felt the same way. Perhaps like the rich young ruler he went away dejected at the cost of Jesus' demands. If this is what is expected, "Who then can be saved?" (Luke 18:26b, see vv.18-29). But what is humanly impossible is possible with God, who in human form has gone before us. Jesus once called himself the Good Shepherd. He could also have called himself the Good Samaritan, for he came to us across what was thought an impossible boundary, and he risked and endured misunderstanding, injustice, even atrocity at our hands. And though we killed him, he still loved us. That is the love that overcomes the world; that is the love that overcomes death; that is the love that enables us to love our neighbor as our—naked and helpless—selves. Such love is our hope of glory; may we be found to walk in it.

---

[4]*Brothers Karamazov*, chapter entitled, "Rebellion."

We see white and black, Lord.
We see white teeth in a black face,
We see black eyes in a white face.
Help us to see persons, Jesus, not a black person,
or a white person, a red person or a yellow person,
but human persons.[5]

---

[5] A prayer of Malcolm Boyd.

Appendix

Comprehensive Plan: For Integrating North American Ethnic Minority Persons and Their Interests Into Every Facet of Calvin's Institutional Life

Summary

The need for Calvin College to become a genuinely multicultural Christian academic community has been recognized by the Board of Trustees, the Administration and the Faculty of the college. The Comprehensive Plan here presented plots out a course that will make Calvin College the multicultural community here envisioned.

Four critical areas in need of focused attention are identified in the plan: (1) Faculty and Staff—the recruitment and retention of ethnic minority persons and the development of multicultural community; (2) Student Life—the recruitment and retention of ethnic minority students and the development of multicultural student community; (3) The Broader Christian Community; and (4) Curriculum. In each of these areas an account of what the college has done in the past is given, goals for the college are set, and strategies for goal achievement are recommended.

Four themes underlie all the goals and the strategies contained in this plan. First, academic excellence at Calvin will be maintained, and more likely improved, for a multicultural educational community is better than a homogeneous one. Second, change at Calvin is mandatory, something we must do soon and with great resolve. Third, the change must be comprehensive, reaching into all facets of Calvin's institutional life. Fourth, to ensure success the plan is careful to assign, where appropriate, authority and responsibility to specific individuals, divisions, departments, or committees.

Faculty and Staff. In this area the goals are (1) that by the year 2003-04 fifteen percent of both faculty and staff will be comprised of ethnic minority persons, and (2) that faculty and staff will work together in a multicultural Christian community. Recruitment of faculty will be primarily the burden of the various academic departments, but they will be assisted in their efforts by the Director of Academic Multicultural Affairs who will make special efforts at ethnic minority recruitment, and who will also promote faculty exchanges and graduate fellowships for promising ethnic minority graduate students. Administration and staff recruitment and retention will be the primary responsibility of the various college divisions, but they will be assisted by a personnel manager in charge of various recruitment and retention programs. The development of multicultural community will be guided by the Multicultural Affairs Committee, which will encourage community building activities wherever appropriate.

Student Life. The goals in this section are (1) that by the year 2003-04 fifteen percent of the student body will be comprised of ethnic minority students, (2) that retention figures for ethnic minority students will not differ from those of the whole student body, and (3) that students of all ethnic origins will live and study together in Christian community. Success in this area requires that the admissions development office strengthen recruitment efforts, that the student affairs division work to improve multicultural community living in on-campus housing, and that the Multicultural Affairs Committee encourage and ensure positive cross-cultural communication in various student arenas. Success here also requires the appointment of a Director of Student Multicultural Development to the student affairs division. This director will advise ethnic minority students and will generally work to foster an environment in which cross-cultural community is celebrated.

The Broader Christian Community. The goals here are (1) that Calvin will be seen as a credible witness of the culturally diverse character of the Kingdom of God, and (2) that Calvin will build bridges of communication and cooperation with ethnic minority communities. The Multicultural Affairs Committee will be charged with developing and recommending strategies for Calvin's leadership in this area. In addition, because the Board of Trustees is one link Calvin has to the broader Christian community, we recommend that the Board evaluate and define its role in the development of multicultural community both at Calvin and in the broader community.

Curriculum. Our goal for the development of the curriculum is that Calvin graduates will know and appreciate cultures other than those dominant in North America and Western Europe, and that they will be prepared to interact effectively with people from cultures other than their own. The primary strategy is for the college to establish a distribution requirement which will ensure that all students complete a minimum number of courses which provide significant exposure to cultures other than those dominant in North America and Western Europe. The academic administration is charged with encouraging departments and individual faculty to develop or improve such courses.

This is a Comprehensive Plan. It attempts to address issues of importance in all significant areas of Calvin College's institutional life. Still, not all issues are addressed in the same degree of detail. Some of the plan (e.g. faculty recruitment strategies) is well advanced while other parts (e.g. strategies for leadership in the broader Christian community) are in early stages of development. In the coming years this plan will serve to guide change at Calvin. It is meant to be a beginning. The final goal will be achieved only when such plans are no longer necessary.

Vision for the Future

The need for Calvin College to become a genuinely multicultural Christian academic community has been recognized by the Board of Trustees, the Administration and the Faculty of the college. This recognition is underscored by several efforts in the last fifteen or twenty years to increase the presence of ethnic minority faculty and students as well as to orient the curriculum to issues of ethnic minority interest. The Comprehensive Plan here presented takes account of past successes and failures in these areas and plots out a course that will make Calvin College the multicultural community here envisioned.

The vision is of a Christian community that celebrates cultural diversity and is shaped by the biblical vision of the kingdom of God, a kingdom formed ". . . from every tribe and language and people and nation" (Revelation 5:9, 10). We envision a kingdom community in which cultural diversity is seen as normal; a Christian "family" that transcends ethnic, cultural, racial, and class boundaries: a communion of saints in which "each member should consider it his duty to use his gifts readily and cheerfully for the service and enrichment of the other members" (Lord's Day 21 of the Heidelberg Catechism); a community in which Reformed Christians from all of these groups see Calvin as *their* college. It is the biblical vision of Pentecost rather than the vision of Babel.

As an institution under the Lordship of Christ, Calvin College has a prophetic role to play in bearing witness to that kingdom. Central to this prophetic role is the content and orientation of our teaching. More importantly, however, the reality of the kingdom must also be portrayed by the make-up of the educational community, and by the quality of relationships in that community. As long as Calvin remains a one-race, one-culture institution in which the few ethnic minority persons present are isolated by our insensitivity, we present a distorted or, at best, incomplete portrait of the kingdom of God. If we at Calvin assent to the contemporary confession *Our World Belongs to God* and "commit ourselves to seeking and expressing the unity of all who follow Jesus" and become "human family together—male and female, red, yellow, black, white or brown, young, or old" (Paragraphs 47.16) then Calvin College, with resurrection power and anticipatory radiance, will faithfully reflect God's kingdom on earth.

Calvin College is currently far from realizing this vision. In practical terms, we in the Calvin College community must recognize that ethnic minority faculty and ethnic minority students do not feel comfortable here. Among the consequences of this are that the quality of the education of all Calvin students is diminished, the Christian liberal arts education about which we feel so strongly becomes more difficult for ethnic minority Christians to obtain, and the potential for ethnic minority leadership development is diminished. The time for Calvin to change has come. This plan is meant to be a beginning. The final goal will be achieved only when such plans are no longer necessary.

About the Contributors

Glandion Carney is minister at Centrepointe Church, Grand Rapids, Michigan.

Joel Carpenter is Provost of Calvin College.

Justo González is Executive Director of the Theological Hispanic Initiative in Decatur, Georgia.

David Hoekema is Academic Dean and Professor of Philosophy at Calvin College.

Michelle Loyd-Paige is Associate Professor of Sociology at Calvin College.

Caesar Molebatsi is Director of Youth Alive Development Corporation in Johannesburg, South Africa.

Chris Stoffel Overvoorde is Professor emeritus of Art at Calvin College.

Cornelius Plantinga Jr. is Dean of the Chapel and Adjunct Professor of Religion and Theology at Calvin College.

Richard Plantinga is Associate Professor of Religion and Theology at Calvin College.

Thomas Thompson is Associate Professor of Religion and Theology at Calvin College.

Steven Timmermans is Dean for Instruction and Associate Professor of Education at Calvin College.

Leanne Van Dyk is Associate Professor of Theology at San Francisco Theological Seminary.